Tantra For

Tantra For Westerners
A Practical Guide to the Way of Action

Francis X King

Mandrake

Published by

Mandrake of Oxford

PO Box 250

OXFORD

OX1 1AP (UK)

CONTENTS

INTRODUCTION
Tantra—The Way of Action

It is perfectly correct to describe Tantra as 'an unorthodox religious tendency to be found in Jainism, Hinduism and Buddhism.'

It is equally correct to describe it as 'a mystical system concerned with polarity in general and sexuality in particular.'

But both descriptions are incomplete. While Tantra has mystical, philosophical, and religious aspects it is, above all, a technique of *action*—a physical, mental, and spiritual discipline which incorporates meditation, yoga, and sacramental worship in the very widest sense of that phrase.

All the actions undertaken by a practitioner of Tantra are performed with one purpose only; they are all means to the same end. That end is the transformation of the individual, his or her rebirth to a new existence on every level of consciousness.

There is no 'tantric faith', to be accepted or rejected on the bases of thought and emotion; the philosophy, cosmology, and psychology of Tantra certainly exist—but they are no more than hypotheses which explain, reasonably satisfactorily, the results which are achieved by the performance of certain processes.

Tantra makes precisely the same claim as that made by ritual magic: 'If you follow a certain course of action with dedication and persistence you will be led back to the roots of your own identity, you will learn the truth about yourself and the universe which you inhabit, and the nature of your existence will be transformed.'

Too many Westerners who have attempted to test the truth of these assertions for themselves have failed, or abandoned the attempt in despair, because they have followed the letter rather than the spirit of Tantra. They have felt, for example, that they cannot carry out the Ritual of the Five Ms (details of which are given at a later stage) unless they first obtain some unusual variety of parched grain which is not easily available outside India.

In reality, however, there is nothing specifically Indian, or even oriental, about the processes which are the central core of Tantra, and symbolism expressing those processes can be discerned in both ancient Sumerian carvings and in European cave paintings which date from the Stone Age.

There is no reason why Europeans or Americans should not practise Tantra at the same time as following a way of life perfectly compatible with the societies in which they live, in this way finding out for themselves whether or not Tantra is, as its adepts claim, a way of Liberation.

Tantra for Westerners provides a practical guide to the way in which this can be done.

CHAPTER ONE

Pleasure and Pain

The late Luis Bunuel's film *La Voie Lactée* was the first—and will probably be the last—attempt to explore the history of unorthodox Christianity in terms of art cinema.

Two tramps hitchhike along 'the Milky Way', the route which medieval French pilgrims followed on their pious journeying towards the Spanish shrine of St James of Compostella.

On their way many remarkable things happen to them. They encounter Satan, who gives one of them a comfortable pair of shoes to relieve his blistered feet. They see the sudden conversion of a Catholic priest to eccentric sacramental doctrines as the result of eating a particularly delicious hare pâté. Oddest of all, they are subjected to sudden temporal displacements, being hurled back into the past, where they witness many curious events, amongst them an unorthodox celebration of Mass, which takes place at night in a clearing in the woods with bare-breasted women being given huge lumps of leavened bread by the celebrant priest.

This episode, which cinema audiences seem to have found even more puzzling than the rest of the film, was intended as a portrayal of the activities of Priscillian, a fourth-century Spanish Bishop who was executed for sorcery in AD 386.

Priscillian was alleged to have taught that physical matter (including the human body) was intrinsically evil, the creation of Satan and, as such, inherently incapable of 'becoming holy'. It could be used, however, as a means of *attaining* sanctification—using evil to overcome evil. The flesh, it was averred, was so different from the spirit that the fleshly and spiritual must be totally divorced from one another if the spirit was to attain liberation. Thus matrimony was rejected as a futile attempt to sanctify the body and its fleshly desires, resulting only in the spirit becoming ever more fully trapped in the body. Free love, on the other hand, was acceptable provided it involved only the lusts of the body, while the spirit, the Divine Spark in each human being, was kept detached and uninvolved in physical sexuality.

Whether Priscillian did or did not believe in this extraordinary version of dualistic theology is uncertain. As is the case with most heretical thinkers of his times, none of his writings survive[1] and his teachings are only known through the distorted accounts given by his opponents.

Nevertheless, there seems no doubt that the erotic activities of Priscillian and his congregation were unusual—that they were representative of an unorthodox mystical undercurrent the presence of which can be detected in most of the world's great religions, from Christianity to Hinduism, from Islam to Buddhism.

This undercurrent can perhaps best be described as 'mystical hedonism'—the use of the pleasures of physical existence as a technique of psychic and spiritual transformation, the use of the senses to *overcome* the senses.

For reasons which will be explained later, the detailed history of this mystical undercurrent in all its many aspects (of which Hindu and Buddhist tantrism are the most fully developed) will never be known. It is clear, however, that it represents an abiding tradition. The current is normally beneath the surface, its very existence unsuspected save by those who have voluntarily immersed themselves in it. But its continuation is proved by the fact that from time to time it breaks forth from its confines and surges into full view, surprising and alarming the general population—the orthodox of every faith.

Thus, for example, the leaders of German Lutheranism were horrified when, in the late seventeenth century, the undergound tradition manifested itself in the form of a Pietist community. The leader of the community was a certain Eva von Buttlar; it is not unusual, for reasons which will be made apparent in the succeeding chapter, for women to be prominent in hedonistic mystical movements. Eva von Buttlar, the aristocratic wife of a French steward at the Court of Eisenach, led the ordinary life of a woman of her class until she was twenty-five years old. Then, in 1697, she underwent a process of conversion to mystical Christianity as a result of a combination of interior experiences and a reading of German translations of the writings of the English mystic John Pordage, one-time rector of the Berkshire parish of Bradfield.

As is apparent from Pordage's writings there were two main literary influences on his mystical philosophy. The first, and more obvious, was Jacob Boehme; the second was the Jewish mystical system known

---

1. Certain treatises attributed to Priscillian have survived, but they are not authentic, although possibly written by a man strongly influenced by Priscillian's teachings.

as qabalism. It is probable that what Pordage knew of the qabalah was entirely derived from secondary sources—the writings of Christian commentators upon the subject—but it seems to me likely that Pordage's concept of *Sophia* (the eternal feminine principle of Virgin Wisdom) owes quite as much to the Shekinah of the qabalists as it does to Boehme.

Eva von Buttlar became intoxicated with *Sophia*, experiencing trances in which she entered—or, at any rate, believed that she entered—a unitive state with the Virgin Wisdom. So profound was the psychological effect of these trances that she came to see herself as a physical incarnation of Wisdom—the 'Second Eve' in a precisely similar sense to that in which St Paul regarded Christ as the 'Second Adam.' Such beliefs were, so it would seem, founded on an inadequate psychological understanding of the mystical experience of union with the archetypal Great Mother (the Shakti of tantrism) and, almost inevitably, led to a rejection of accepted social and sexual conventions; according to the Lutheran opponents of Eva von Buttlar she and her associates not only engaged in unlimited sexual intercourse with one another, but held their property in common and believed that there could be no barriers of rank or wealth between 'brothers and sisters in Christ.' This last was, of course, considered a particularly shocking doctrine in the class-conscious Germany of *c.*1700.

As was the case with the teachings of Priscillian, we only know the doctrines and practices of Eva's community through the accounts, no doubt distorted, of her enemies. There is no real doubt, however, that she was concerned with the use of some sort of technique designed to employ the senses in the service of the spirit—her own reported statements about 'eternal Eve' and 'the eternal androgynous Adam' make this clear enough. [2]

A similar outburst of 'hedonistic mysticism' took place in nineteenth-century France, and aspects of it can be discerned in the writings of the French occultist Eliphas Lévi, in the history of the Vintrasian movement (in particular of that segment of it led by the Abbé Boullan), and in the novels of J. K. Huysmans. Interestingly enough, these latter influenced Archbishop Kowalski, a leading figure in that strangest of twentiety-century erotic/mystical movements, the Mariavite Church of Poland.

A detailed account of Mariavitism is outside the scope of this book.

---

2. For an account of the life and teachings of Eva von Buttlar see Volume 2 of M. Goebel's historical study of the Rhine-Westphalian Evangelical Church (Coblenz, 1855). See also Nils Thune's *The Behmenists and the Philadelphians* (Uppsala, 1948).

It suffices to say that the movement began as an expression of extreme Catholicism, 'more Roman than the Vatican', and ended as an independent ecclesiastical body in which priestesses and 'female Bishops' were dominant. Many of these latter engaged in sexual activities with their leader, Archbishop Kowalski; some of them believed that they also had similar relationships with saints and angels.[3]

The Mariavites were in many ways an unimpressive example of the hedonist-mystical tradition; they were anti-intellectual, credulous, and had an unpleasantly exclusivist attitude, regarding those who did not share their curious beliefs as being 'blotted out from the Book of Life' and doomed to eternal fire. What, however, is significant about the Mariavite movement is that it emerged, and, for a time, flourished, in an extremely unfavourable environment—the conservative peasant-society of ultra-Catholic Poland. That the undercurrent manifested itself in such a situation shows its strength. Mariavitism may have been a flawed mirror, but it reflected, albeit distortedly, an image of terrifying archetypal power.

All mystical and magical techniques can be divided into two broad categories, the cathartic and the hedonistic. The mainstream of the mystical tradition follows the way of catharsis, or purging. That is to say, its techniques are aimed at the purification of the individual by purging him or her of 'earthly things'; humanity is regarded as a mixture of gold and dross, and the way of mystic attainment is looked upon as a progressive refinement of the gold from the dross. In practice this means a withdrawal from the world and its pleasures—food, drink, warmth, sexual satisfaction, and so on. In short, the way of the cathartic mystic, be he Muslim, Hindu, or Christian, is some form of asceticism.

In the final analysis, the counter-tradition of hedonistic religion, mysticism, and magic also rejects the world of the flesh, which it regards as only a pale reflection of underlying reality. Its exponents believe, however, that it is possible to use the things which please the senses in order to *transcend* those senses. They argue that supernormal modes of consciousness—including, eventually, the supreme unitive experience—can be attained through the correct use and understanding of the pleasures of the flesh. The hedonistic tradition eschews the pains of asceticism for the pleasures of the body; it pursues spiritual liberation through life affirmation, not physical restriction.

This tradition, as has already been made clear, has survived in the Western world as an undercurrent running far beneath the surface of orthodoxy. In the truest sense it has been an occult—that is, a secret—

---

3. For a detailed, scholarly, and intensely readable account of Mariavitism see *The Third Adam* (OUP, 1978) by Jerzey Peterkiewicz.

tradition, finding its expression in eccentric religion, in some aspects of alchemy, and, above all, in ritual magic. Undoubtedly the purest forms of this hedonistic tradition are to be found in Jain, Buddhist, and Hindu Tantra. In the course of this book detailed accounts are given of both the ritual and meditative techniques employed in Tantra and the cosmological, philosophical, psychological, and anatomical theories which are associated with the use of those same techniques. It should be noted that the latter, the theories and beliefs associated with Tantra, are *not* primary. In other words, Tantra is a mode of action, not a system of beliefs or a way of thought—the theoretical structures associated with the use of the techniques are merely attempts to explain the results of using them.

Whether they are Buddhists, Hindus, or Jains, all adepts of Tantra view both the universe and the individuals who inhabit it as being composed of pairs of polar opposites—male and female, static and dynamic, soft and hard, negative and positive, and so on.

The existence of these opposites, their intrinsic duality, is considered to be the source of all change and of sorrow and suffering, the twin children of change. The ultimate aim of each human being's spiritual strivings should be, so it is held, an escape from the world of duality into an existence (in Buddhism non-existence) in which the opposites are transformed into a higher unity—a state in which the very concept of polarity has become meaningless. The similarities between this and the Hegelian triad of thesis, antithesis, and synthesis are clear. Such similarities, however, must not be overstressed. The synthesis of Hegel (and Karl Marx) was seen as itself becoming a thesis with an antithesis, and thus an element in a new polarity. The tantric 'slaying of opposites' is seen as being as final as anything can be—for the individual who has achieved it is regarded as being emancipated from polarity 'until the worlds become voidness and new worlds manifest'.

Hindu tantrics term the negative element of polarity, which is regarded as being male, Shiva, thus identifying it with the most popular diety of the present-day Hindu pantheon. The dynamic element, considered to be female, is called Shakti. Every thing or being which exists, from molecules of dust to stars, from bacteria to archangels, is held to contain elements of both Shiva and Shakti. The Shakti element in humanity is symbolized as a serpent (Kundalini) which, in the unenlightened, lies coiled and sleeping at the base of the spine; Shiva is conceived as 'living' above the crown of the Head. The techniques of Tantra involve a great deal of what might be called 'spiritual shock therapy'. Before considering the nature and purpose of this it is well to take account of similar processes in other mystical systems.

Mystical teachers of almost every tradition have used shock to

stimulate their pupils, to jerk the mental processes of those pupils out
of their accustomed pathways, thus inducing a temporary dissociation
of consciousness which enables the acceptance of new concepts, new
ways of regarding the self and its environment.

To induce such dissociation-by-shock Taoist masters have ordered
their pupils to perform tasks which are not only pointless but incapable
of achievement. Similarly, some ascetics have indulged in grossly sensual
activities in full sight of their disciples, while pious Sufis have loudly
announced that the Koran contains nothing but nonsensical lies.

In the Tantra of India such shock tactics are to be found in a highly
systematized and, from the point of view of psychology, violent form.
The central observances of Tantra are profoundly sinful to an orthodox
Hindu; it is no exaggeration to say that they are as alien to the normal
usages of Indian life as the ritual consumption of pork in Mecca would
be to the normal usages of Islamic pilgrimage. 'I shall proclaim', says
one Bengali tantric text, '... the supreme religious experience, following
the performance of which the adept speedily gains magical powers in
this Black Era. The rosary should be made of human teeth, the cup
of a man's brain-pan ... the sacrificial ingredients are to be saturated
with wine, one must have sexual relationship with another's wife, no
matter what her caste ...' The mere *reading* of such injunctions, let
alone carrying them out, is enough to induce a feeling of profound
disturbance in the mind of an orthodox Hindu.

The final purpose of the activities recommended in the passage quoted
above is not to gain the 'magical powers' mentioned in the text. It is
to induce the serpent of Shakti to arouse herself from the slumbers
in which she lies coiled at the base of the spine, to raise herself through
the subtle energy pathways associated with the spine, and to unite herself
with Shiva. This divine marriage of opposing polarities will, so it is
believed, destroy inner duality and liberate the tantric adept from the
effects of pain, suffering and change.

In the Tantra of Bengal (which is now practised in many other parts
of India) the Ceremony of the Five Ms is employed as the easiest way
of arousing Shakti from sleep. The Five Ms are: *matsya*, fish; *mamsa*,
which really means any sort of meat but in this context usually signifies
beef, totally forbidden to a Hindu of any caste; *madya*, wine, arak, or
some other alcoholic drink; *mudra*, which word in tantric terminology
usually means parched grain or dried beans but can be applied to almost
any vegetable substance supposedly possessed of aphrodisiac virtues;
and *maithuna*, sexual intercourse.

As a preliminary to the Ceremony of the Five Ms tantric addicts
often take some preparation derived from cannabis. This, it must be
emphasized, is *not* part of the rite, nor even an essential prelude to the

rite. Exactly why it is so often used has been a subject of debate amongst students of Tantra, but it seems very likely that the social conventions of Indian life are so strong that most tantrics would be unable to break its rigid taboos (such as that against eating beef) unless they first dulled normal consciousness, thus overcoming inhibition, by the use of an hallucinogenic drug.

The ceremony proper begins with prayers of exactly the same nature as those used in conventional Hinduism; following these the fish, meat, wine, and reputedly aphrodisiac vegetables are consumed. In a certain sense, however, the tantric adept does not *really* eat or drink these forbidden substances. For as the food and drink are swallowed the idea is held in the mind that it is Shakti, the dynamic cosmic principle, to which nothing can be alien or unholy, which is simply taking back into itself physical matter which, like every other aspect of the manifested universe, is a by-product of the continual interplay of Shiva and Shakti.

Maithuna, sexual intercourse, is the culmination of the rite. The male adept draws a triangular diagram, symbolizing Shakti, on his couch or sleeping mat, lays his partner upon it, and then, visualizing her as Shakti and himself as Shiva, commences what is usually a lengthy copulation. Throughout this, mantras—rhythmic phrases of supposed mystical significance and power—are endlessly repeated. A specific mantra is used at each stage of the lovemaking, the holiest being reserved for the moment of orgasm.

To this ceremony is attributed a remarkable efficacy. As one text expresses it, 'the adept who follows this path becomes a great poet, a Lord of the Earth, and goes forth mounted upon an elephant'. In ancient India, of course, 'riding an elephant' was symbolic of power, wisdom, and even kingliness.

It should be noted that there is a variant of the Ceremony of the Five Ms in which very little happens on a physical level, the rite being largely carried out in the form of pictorial mental imagery—as a western occultist might put it, 'the working is almost exclusively astral'.

This type of symbolic ritual is employed in 'right-handed' Tantra; that in which the workings are physical is known as 'left-handed' Tantra. The terms left and right as used in Tantra have no moral overtones whatsoever; it must not be thought that the term 'left-handed Tantra' in any way equates with what Western occultists call 'the left-hand path'—i.e. Satanism and Black Magic. The terms 'left-handed' and 'right handed' Tantra merely express the fact that in the early stage of ceremonies culminating in physical sexuality the female adept sits on the left hand of the male, while in symbolic ceremonies she sits on the right.

In a later chapter of this book the techniques of Tantra are examined in the light of what the late Dion Fortune described as 'the Western Esoteric Tradition' (i.e. the syncretic magical/mystical system created by S. L. MacGregor Mathers and his associates), and some consideration is given as to how, and to what extent, tantric methods can be advantageously applied by Western mystics and magicians. It is, however, worth holding in mind that the essence of Tantra is the use of the senses as a way of transcending sensuality and achieving 'liberation', 'enlightenment', 'Divine Union', call it what you will. No particular rite, meditation, posture, or mantra is of the essence of Tantra—they are all merely very partial expressions of that essence, applicable at a certain place and time, but not elsewhere or elsewhen. Thus, for example, many of the features of the Ceremony of the Five Ms lack any shock-value whatsoever for most Westerners—for them, drinking wine and eating beef are perfectly commonplace activities and no cultural or psychic shock is induced by the concept of cow killing.

CHAPTER TWO
Power and Passivity

As was pointed out earlier, Tantra is above all a Way of Action, a pragmatic system which, in the final analysis, stands or falls on whether it *works*. In other words, individuals who experiment with Tantra must decide whether it is true *for them*, whether it does, or does not, produce the psychic transformations which its adepts have claimed that it produces.

The central core of Tantra is a technique, or, rather a number of closely interrelated techniques. Around this core has developed a body of mystical philosophy, psychology, and even physiology, which can be regarded as epiphenomenal, i.e. as 'side effects' produced by the phenomena, these being the physical, mental, and spiritual transformations which supposedly result from the use of the core techniques.

The 'side effects' have become so closely associated with the core from which they are derived that it is impossible to study one without the other, for although the practice gave birth to the theory, and is thus 'primary Tantra', the theory has undoubtedly exerted some influence upon the practice. This body of theory is, of course, concerned with the polarity symbolized in the continual embrace of Shiva and Shakti, the static and dynamic aspects of the cosmos.

A question must inevitably arise as to the validity of the mystical philosophy of Tantra. That question must not be anything so simple—and unanswerable—as 'Is the polarity of philosophy of Tantra true or false', but 'Is the polarity philosophy of Tantra in accordance with the inmost nature of humanity?'

This latter question is more complex than it may appear to be at first sight, and other questions are hidden within it. Two of these implicit questions are as follows:

1. Is the mystical philosophy of Tantra, however internally consistent

it may be, no more than an artificial construct built on the basis
of unproved and unprovable axioms—a mystical counterpart of
the internally consistent non-Euclidean geometrics which can be
built on the basis of such axioms as 'a line is never the shortest
distance between two points'?

2. Or is the philosophy of Tantra an expression of a human reality—a
    basic polarity (or, at least, duality) which can be discerned in every
    aspect of human activity, from breathing to copulation, from feeling
    to reasoning, from dying to undergoing the pangs of spiritual rebirth?

Before considering the first question it is best to attempt to answer
the second.

Duality is perhaps the most obvious characteristic of human anatomy
and physiology. Externally this is apparent at the merest glance—a man
or woman who has only one eye, or one leg, or even one nostril, is
clearly marred, incomplete, the victim of genetic or environmental
damage. Internally the same twoness manifests itself in many of the
vital organs; we have two kidneys, there are two chambers to the heart,
and, consequently, there is a polarity between arterial and venous blood;
normally men have two testicles and women have two ovaries; the
brain is divided into two hemispheres, and so on.

There is no need to posit any great occult or mystic significance to
this dominant duality, which clearly has enormous evolutionary
advantages—the damage or destruction of a single kidney, for example,
does not mean the destruction of the body of which it forms a part,
for a single healthy kidney can carry out the work normally performed
by two. What is significant, however, is that on the level of form, the
human body, like that of all mammalian bodies, is an expression of
'twoness'. Whether this duality is the outcome of chance or design,
the product of random mutation or the activities of a Creator, is totally
irrelevant to the fact that it exists.

It could well be objected that this physical duality is no more than
that, i.e. it is not a polarity of the sort with which Tantra is concerned.
Such an objection is reasonable enough; one kidney is the twin of the
other, not its polar opposite, the right lung performs precisely the same
task as the left one, and so on. But with at least some pairs of organs
one can discern a slight functional differentiation, a sort of proto-
polarity—in tantric terminology, the faintest reflection of the everlasting
coupling of Shiva and Shakti—which results in a qualitative
improvement in the functioning of the pair. Take, for example, the eyes.
The field of vision of a one-eyed man would not be greatly enlarged
if he was given a second eye, but he would experience a change in
the quality of his vision, for he would perceive objects in three

dimensions, instead of the two possible with monocular sight. Such proto-polarity in human biology can be extended to a full polarity, a complete expression of the Shiva/Shakti duality, if the functions of the physical body are analysed in accordance with the principles of the system of alternative medicine developed by Dr Ita Wegman, Dr Lili Kolisko, Dr A. Leroi, and other physicians and scientists who have been influenced by the life and thought of Rudolf Steiner (1864-1925).

According to the practitioners and devotees of this system the structure and development of the human biosystem can only be satisfactorily interpreted in terms of polarities and 'third principles' through which they relate to one another. Ita Wegman and her associates, 'anthroposophical physicians', asserted that the life of the individual was an interplay between the cephalic pole and its instrument, the nerve-sense system, and the metabolic pole, sometimes referred to as the 'motor-digestive pole'. The cephalic pole is concerned with feeling, thought, and consciousness; the metabolic pole with mobility, willing, digestion, and excretion—both forms of movement. There is, so it is believed, a dialectical interplay between the two poles; everything which takes place at the cephalic pole, i.e. nerve-sense processes such as sight, hearing, and taste, influences the metabolic pole, and vice versa. Thus, for example, when a hungry man imagines the meal he plans to eat shortly a nerve-sense process is taking place, but the metabolic pole immediately becomes involved and the stomach is made ready to carry out the processes of digestion.

Whether or not this anthroposophical conception of human polarity is of any practical medical value is uncertain, although there is no doubt that many thousands of men and women claim to have benefited from the use of holistic anthroposophic therapies of which the underlying rationale—an attempt to restore a balance between the nerve-sense and motor-digestive systems—is to be found in the polarity theories expounded by Rudolf Steiner and his associates.

Quite apart from the question of the objective truth or falsehood of anthroposophical and other conceptions about polarity, it would seem that there is some element in the psychological structure of human beings which finds it intellectually and emotionally *satisfying* to classify the various aspects of reality in terms of pairs of opposites. Both now and in the past men and women have had a 'bias in favour of duality', an instinctive feeling that 'twoness' was somehow *right*.

This bias neither is, nor ever has been, confined to those, such as anthroposophists, who have been influenced by mystical and occult traditions. Perhaps the most remarkable (certainly the most soporific) example of an attempt to classify every aspect and process of phenomenal existence in terms of conflicts between pairs of opposites was provided by Friedrich Engels, the collaborator and paymaster of Karl Marx, when he wrote his *Dialectics of Nature*, a work whose serialization in the German socialist newspaper *Vörwarts* resulted in widespread complaints and a catastrophic fall in circulation.

It has been suggested that our human predilection for twoness is biological, originating from the fact that there are only two sexes. If, so it has been argued, there were four or five different genders involved in the reproductive process we would tend to think in fours or fives, rather than twos. In this case we would not, for example, think of human actions as 'good' or 'evil', a simple polarity, but instead have four or five different ethical categories, to one or other of which any individual action would be attributed.

It is possible that there is some truth in this reductionist approach; sexuality is the most obvious example of a Shiva/Shakti polarity. But the underlying duality, the division into pairs of opposites, is visible in every aspect of nature and, to some extent, seems built into the physical structure of the universe. Any particle of matter above the sub-atomic level with which quantum theory is concerned is either present in a particular area of space or it is not; any creature built up of protoplasm is either alive or it is dead; either an electrical current is flowing through a circuit or it is not; and, whether or not existence is a predicate, anything of which we can conceive either exists or it is non-existent.

Our primitive ancestors were unconcerned with electrical currents and predicates, but they sensed an inherent duality in life and its surroundings. The course of natural events on earth is for night to succeed day, for the harvest to eventually follow the sowing of the seed, for the tide to ebb and flow, and so on. The lives of individual men and women show the same pendulum-like swing between opposing polarities such as sleep and waking, activity and rest, love and hate, fertility and barrenness, and birth and death.

Our ancestors were quite as aware, perhaps more aware, of these natural polarities, interior and exterior, as we are ourselves. It is not surprising, therefore, that many primitive creation myths are concerned with duality, typically the separation of darkness from light, or the cosmic copulation of the Sky Father with the Earth Mother. Thus, for example, the early Sumerians believed that earthly life originated from the coupling of Enki, a god particularly associated with fresh water, and the goddess Ninhursag, 'the Mother of the Land'. Similarly, the ancient Babylonians held that there had been two elements of the primordial chaos, Tiamat and Apsu, from whom all the gods, including Marduk the creator of earth, were generated. The creation myth associated with the ancient Egyptian cultus of Atum is particularly interesting, for it depends upon a whole series of divine polarities, all ultimately derived from autosexual activity.

Atum, the primal god—some modern occultists have identified him with the Ain Soph of the qabalists—was believed to have engaged in an act of masturbation, from his semen springing a god and goddess, Shu and Tefnut, who immediately engaged in copulation. Their twin children, Geb, identified with the earth, and Nuit, the sky, were themselves the parents of two other divine polarities, Isis and Osiris, Set and Nephthys. The eternal relationship between Nuit and Geb is precisely the same as that between the Shakti and Shiva of Tantra, as is made clear by an illustration to the British Museum's Papyrus of Tamenill, which dates from about 1000 BC. It shows Nuit, supported by the tips of her fingers and toes, arched like a fully flexed bow, vaulting over the body of her brother Geb. In the place where an arrow might be expected is the enormous fully tumescent phallus of Geb, who writhes in ecstasy beneath her.

If the writings of C. G. Jung are to be believed the existence of such creation myths as those described above are far more than primitive attempts to explain creation in terms of sexual generation. They still, averred Jung, speak to us today, for they are mythological expressions of a psychic fact, that a perception of duality is inherent in the structure and conscious processes of the human mind. The essence of the conscious mind, said Jung, is discrimination, the separation of things into pairs of opposites. Without such discrimination there can be no awareness, no consciousness. In the Unconscious the opposites are united—in tantric terminology, Shiva and Shakti are in orgasmic union—but as soon as consciousness begins to manifest itself the contraries split asunder, as the primal 'nothingness' split asunder at the Creation. 'Every act of dawning consciousness', Jung wrote, 'is a creative act, and it is from this psychological experience that all our cosmogonic symbols are derived.'

Jung believed that the key to psychic health was what he called 'individuation', the marriage of the opposites in a union which transcends the contraries, and he interpreted many alchemical texts in terms of a symbolic description of such a process. It is quite certain that in *Psychology and Alchemy* Jung overstated his case. There is no doubt that at least some of the alchemical writings, the meaning of which Jung interpreted as descriptions of interior, psychic processes, were, in fact, concerned with perfectly ordinary laboratory manipulations of physical substances. Nevertheless, it must be admitted that much alchemical literature shows a concern with polarity which is reminiscent of both Tantra and Jung's concept of 'individuation' as a conjoining of opposites.

The Philosophers' Stone, that medicine which will 'give life eternal' and transform lead into gold, is described in language which is paradoxical in its conjunction of opposites. The Stone is not a stone, its origin is divine and earthly, the substance from which it is prepared is enormously expensive and yet regarded as worthless. The conjunction of opposites, implied in a common alchemical description of the Stone as 'made of Fire and Water', is made explicit in some descriptions of what may or not have been laboratory processes. The 'Red Lion' is to be married to the 'White Eagle', the King to the Queen, and the Sun to the Moon. Or the dragon 'must enter the womb of the Mother' or the father 'copulate with the daughter'.

This is polarity symbolism and, what is more, specifically *sexual* polarity symbolism of a type very similar to that encountered in the literature of Tantra. Whether such alchemical symbolism expresses laboratory processes or, as Jung believed, an interior process of individuation, or, indeed, an 'alchemy of sexual fluids' similar to that employed by Taoist adepts, is comparatively unimportant. What is significant is that the authors of much alchemical literature chose to express themselves in terms of sexual polarity; some element in the human psyche impelled alchemists to use polarity symbolism as a way of conveying hidden meanings.

There is no need to assume that these alchemical writers were fully conscious of what they are doing. It is perfectly possible to use specifically sexual symbols without being aware of it. Thus the tarot, the 'wicked pack of cards' of T. S. Eliot, incorporates a good deal of near-tantric polarity symbolism which most of its devotees seem to disregard—on a conscious level. Some of this tarot symbolism is of much interest in the context of a western approach to Tantra, and should therefore be considered in detail.

Before doing so, however, it is essential to deal with some tarot legends and misconceptions which are still surprisingly widespread in occult circles. There are a great many of these tarot myths and legends, all of them historically worthless, although some of them may, like traditional fairy stories, express 'psychic truths'. Such legends typically concern the origins of the tarot, which are said to be found in the Mysteries of Egypt, or in the doctrines of Hebrew qabalism, or even in the esoteric teachings of the spiritual leaders of ancient India. Associated with these beliefs in the antiquity of the tarot is the idea that there is some numerological significance in the fact that the tarot pack used by contemporary occultists contains 22 'greater trumps' and 56 'lesser trumps', 78 cards in all. In fact, however, while many tarot packs, old and new, are made up of 78 cards this is not always the case. Packs of greater or lesser size have been manufactured in the past and some, notably the Sicilian tarot, are still in production. It is true, however, that what has been the most common variety of tarot pack since *c*.1750 consists of 78 cards, and that this has been the deck which has fascinated such diverse personalities as P. D. Ouspensky, Aleister Crowley, and W. B. Yeats.

While the precise date of the designs of the pack which is the ancestor of the present-day 'occult tarot' is still uncertain, it is an undoubted fact that no contemporary historian of either playing cards or European art history would argue that the tarot existed in anything like its present form before the fourteenth century AD. It also seems certain that the prototypes of modern tarot packs were designed in southern Europe, not in Egypt or India. Yet those long-dead students of the tarots who discerned in it the symbols of ancient Egyptian religion, of qabalism, and of the Shiva/Shakti cultus of Tantra were no fools; they produced what seemed to be strong supporting evidence in favour of their theories. They had quite correctly observed that the symbolism of the tarot seemed to reflect the symbol systems of, and be in harmony with, the qabalah, classical Mystery cults, and of the Tantra of ancient Hindustan.

No one who has 'worked', through either meditation or divination, with the symbols of the occult tarot pack can have much doubt that the perceived harmony is a psychic reality. Yet it is a virtual certainty that the man, or men, who originally devised the tarot were totally unacquainted with any of the symbol systems with which the tarot is in harmony.

There are two possible methods of resolving this paradox.

The first is one to which many Western occultists have been inclined—the devisers of the tarot deck were, quite literally, inspired. According to this hypothesis no ordinary human being could have been capable of constructing the elaborate, and internally consistent, symbolic structure of the tarot without, in the words of Crowley, 'the assistance of superiors whose mental processes were, and are, pertaining to a higher Dimension.' These supposed 'superiors . . . pertaining to a higher Dimension' were, of course, those whom Theosophists term the Masters or Mahatmas—the 'Secret Chiefs' of the Golden Dawn and similar esoteric societies.

The second hypothesis which explains the remarkable concordance between tarot symbolism and various systems of mystical philosophy is that of the existence of what the mystics and magicians of the Renaissance called *Anima Mundi*, 'the Soul of the World'.

Anima Mundi is conceived of as being the totality of the world's experiences, a sort of 'planetary memory' in which everything that has ever happened on earth is preserved for all time. The 'happenings' preserved include not only physical events but thoughts; everything conceived, at any period of earth's history, in the mind of any living creature, including men and women, is supposedly retained in the depths of *Anima Mundi*. In effect, *Anima Mundi* is to the evolution of mind on our planet as fossils are to the evolution of protoplasm.

Anima Mundi is in some ways analogous to the underground reservoirs of 'fossil water' which exist deep beneath the surface of some of the world's deserts. It is possible to tap these reservoirs; wells can be sunk, fossil water brought to the surface, and new life brought to the barren land. In some places no such effort is required and a spontaneous upwelling from below creates an oasis.

Anima Mundi is a hidden reservoir containing, not water, but images, thoughts and ideas—the collective wisdom of the planet. This reservoir, like reservoirs of fossil water, can be tapped—by the use of meditation, ritual, imagination, and symbol; the living water of *Anima Mundi* can be brought up from the depths below and used to refresh the barren wastes of everyday consciousness. Some men and women can obtain access to the waters of *Anima Mundi* without the use of occult techniques involving magic and meditation. These are artists, poets, all who give free rein to the imaginative faculty and are thus brought, independently and of their own volition, into a state of mind in which symbol and image float upwards into consciousness from the depths of *Anima Mundi*.

On this hypothesis, the artist or artists who designed the tarot pack, perhaps as no more than a gambling game, had sunk so deeply into the 'inner space' of *Anima Mundi* that they had come into contact with the same primitive, and enormously powerful, archetypes which are reflected in the symbols of the qabalah, the Mystery religions of the ancient world and the Tantra of Bengal. In other words, if the ancestor of the modern occult tarot was an authentic work of art, which would seem to have been the case, there is nothing at all surprising in the fact that its symbolism seems to express concepts particularly associated with Tantra.

Symbols consonant with the mystical philosophy and technique of Tantra can be discerned in every one of the 22 Greater Trumps of the tarot, but they are perhaps most noticeable in those entitled Strength, The Star, and The Lovers.

The first of these, Strength, named Force in some packs, is numbered XI in most older tarot packs but VIII in the decks most widely used by Western occultists. All versions of this card show a woman and a lion; usually she is opening or closing his jaws by force, thus showing that the Strength of the card's name refers to her, not, as might be expected, to the lion. In several versions of the card she leads or binds the lion with a chain of flowers, a further emphasis of her dominance, her dynamism as contrasted to the passivity of the lion.

This is pure Tantra; the woman is the dynamic strength of Shakti, the lion is Shiva. In spite of iconographical differences the tarot card entitled Strength is expressing the same concepts as are more explicitly made apparent in Bengali paintings of Shakti energetically dancing upon the prostrate body of Shiva, or in Tibetan yab-yum portrayals of a god and goddess, the latter clearly in violent motion, locked together in ecstatic copulation.

It is interesting to note that the tantric implications of the card were made much more explicit in the tarot deck designed by the late Lady Frieda Harris, an artist whose work was deeply influenced by the complex Gnostic (and, according to some, satanic) intellectualism of Aleister Crowley. Her general approach to the symbolism of this card was indicated by its name being changed from Strength to Lust—Lust, it is to be presumed, in the sense in which the word was used by William Blake when he wrote 'the lust of the goat is the bounty of God', not in the sense that it is used by the makers of X-rated movies.

Lady Harris's card shows a lion with seven heads on which rides a triumphantly and shamelessly naked woman who holds aloft a flaming chalice, a representation of either the Holy Grail or the 'Cup of Abominations' of the Revelation of St John—perhaps both, for Lady Harris, following Crowley, believed that the two were one and the same, and that St John's vision was a distorted one, with beauty appearing under the guise of ugliness and vice versa.[1] The Cup, for Lady Harris, had a tantric import, its significance particularly related to the fivefold Ritual of the Ms, the basic structure of which was described in the preceding chapter. The contents of the Cup, so she believed, was 'the Wine of the Sacrament, the Wine of the Sabbath'—on the most physical level the mingled male and female secretions of the participants in the rites of left-handed Tantra.

Lady Harris was, of course, well aware of the tantric implications of the lion/woman symbolism of the card (Strength) on which her design was based. One can be quite sure that the designer of the original card was not. The significant factor is that the original designer derived from *Anima Mundi* or, if one prefers Jungian terminology, from the depths of the Collective Unconscious, symbols which have tantric implicits.

---

1. The passage of the Revelation of St John which is particularly relevant in this context is to be found in its seventeenth chapter: 'I saw a woman sit upon a scarlet coloured beast, full of names of blasphemy, having seven heads and ten horns. And the woman was arrayed in purple and scarlet colour, and decked with gold and precious stones and pearls, having a golden cup in her hand full of abominations . . .'

The card known as The Lovers has similar implicits. In most older versions it shows a man between two women, above them Cupid, enthroned in the splendour of the noonday sun. In the 'esoteric tarot', used in the original Golden Dawn, the women are, respectively, a whore, and 'a Priestess of the Mysteries' and the man is in a state of inspiration. This design perfectly portrays the dual nature of physical sexuality as conceived by the adepts of Tantra. This duality was referred to by a seventeenth-century Dalai Lama who was reputed to be unchaste. This individual, so it is said, was standing on one of the upper terraces of the great palace of the Potala, listening to the reproaches of his advisers. After politely hearing them out, he gave his reply.

'Yes', he said, 'it is true that I have women, but you who find fault with me also have them, and copulation for me is not the same thing as it is for you.'

In other words, sexual intercourse can be a mere physical indulgence or it can be, as the fifth Dalai Lama claimed was the case with his own couplings, a sacrament, a mode of transcending everyday consciousness. While, no doubt, the Dalai Lama may have been doing no more than making pious excuses for his own pleasures a similar sacramental duality can be discerned in many of the world's religions; wine is usually drunk with no other object than the attainment of bodily pleasure, but it is also sometimes drunk in the belief, right or wrong, that it is a channel of Grace, the veritable Blood of Christ.

The early Golden Dawn version of The Lovers conveys the tantric concept—sex as self-indulgence, sex as sacrament—with admirable clarity and precision. The same is true of the version of the card designed by J. A. Knapp, in which one of the women is portrayed as an angel while the other is 'dishevelled almost to the point of indecency'. Lady Harris, more consciously aware of the elements of Tantra symbolism in the card than any previous designer, concentrated on the angel, sex as sacrament, rather than the harlot, sex as animal activity, and portrayed an 'alchemical marriage'—the Red Lion is being married to the White Eagle and the Black King to the White Queen.

Such alchemical marriages convey tantric polarity symbolism, as was explained on page 22; Lady Harris made the symbolism more explicit, her King bearing a lance, symbolic of the lingam, her Queen bearing a cup, i.e. the yoni as employed in tantric ritual. Once again, it can be seen how the original design of the card incorporated archetypal symbols compatible with Tantra.

The symbolism of the tarot trump entitled The Star reflects the nature of Shakti, the Great Mother, the dynamic, positive aspect of manifestation. The older versions of the card show a naked woman kneeling beside, or sometimes in, a great pool of water. Usually she is poised on one knee, her arms held aloft in such a position that her general posture is vaguely suggestive of a swastika, a symbol which, long before its adoption by the Nazis, was used to represent the dynamic forces of nature. Into the pool she pours water from two vases or, as in the early Golden Dawn version of the card, she pours the contents of one vase over herself, the other into the pool.

According to some interpretations of the meaning of this card the woman must be identified with the Egyptian star-goddess Nuit, who, as suggested on page 21, may be considered to be an analogue of the Shakti of Tantra. In this case the vases are euphemistic images of her ever-flowing breasts, which ceaselessly give forth 'the milk of the stars', the bounty of Shakti, Great Mother of all manifestation.

Reference has been made above to the 'meaning' of tarot cards and it must be emphasized that it is most improbable that such meanings, tantric or otherwise, were consciously present in the minds of the designers of early tarot cards. In a sense these 'meanings' are the creation of modern occultists. This does not mean that such interpretations are necessarily invalid—there are specific problems, of particular importance for students of Tantra, associated with 'the meaning of meaning' in relation to occult texts— 'texts', in this sense, meaning picture-symbols, such as those of the tarot, as well as written material.

The majority of the tantric texts are written on at least two levels, the literal level and the 'real' level. This is because they are written in what is sometimes called 'the twilight language', a sort of code in which ordinary words are given a secondary meaning when used in the context of Tantra. Thus, for example, one Buddhist tantric text instructs its male readers to 'place the *Vajra* in the *padma* but retain the *bodhicitta*'. The literal translation of the word *Vajra* is 'thunderbolt', that of *padma* is 'lotus', while *bodhicitta* has a psychological/philosophical meaning which is very roughly equivalent to the phrase 'mind of enlightenment'. In the twilight language of the school of Tantra which produced this particular work, however, these three words indicate the penis, the vagina, and semen. The instruction, therefore, means 'insert the penis in the vagina and copulate without ejaculation'.

The recognition of two levels of meaning in tantric texts is only, however, a first step towards unravelling their significance. The reader of such texts must, in a sense, engage in a continuous internal dialogue with the text, the 'meaning' of which will develop and change as the reader develops and changes; the text has a personality of its own, it is a teacher which can be asked questions and give answers in the same way as a human teacher.

To accept the existence of such a reader/text dialogue does not demand a total acceptance of any version of structuralist theory. Nevertheless, it is useful to bear in mind Umberto Eco's distinction between the 'closed text' and the 'open text'. The 'closed text', of which an advertisement for soap powder is a good example, conveys only one message, such as 'Buy this brand of soap powder'. The 'open text'—perhaps a novel by Gissing or a poem by Arnold—conveys an *infinity* of meanings. Some of these would have been present, consciously or unconsciously, in the mind of the author of the text, but the remainder are continuously created on the basis of dialogue between reader and text. It must be added that no equation can be made between mass culture and the closed text, or 'high culture' and the open text—popular fairy stories, for example, are good examples of open texts.

Tantric instructional manuals are invariably open texts, and their readers, whether or not they are aware of it, are always engaged in a dialogue with the texts, a dialogue which continually spawns new meanings, potentially as infinite as the body of Shakti itself. The same is true of the texts of other authentic mystical traditions, from alchemy to qabalism, and to criticize as 'unscholarly' those who attach new meanings to old texts—for example, Dion Fortune and Israel Regardie in regard to qabalism—is to miss the essential point.

Having considered the polarity concepts on which the philosophy of Tantra is based in relation to subjects as diverse as human biology, primitive creation myths, alchemy, and the symbolism of the tarot trumps, we are now in a position to arrive at answers to the questions posed on page 18.

Firstly, it is clear that the polarity philosophy of Tantra is not a totally artificial construct, a mystical equivalent of one of the geometries which can be constructed on the basis of non-Euclidean axioms. Secondly, it would seem that polarity is built into the structures of both our minds and bodies, and of the universe in which those minds and bodies have their being. In other words, it is of no great moment whether the philosophy of Tantra represents 'objective truth', if indeed, such a thing exists. For the philosophy of Tantra is *true for us*—polarity is *our* reality, and we can now consider Tantra, the supreme polarity philosophy, in greater detail.

It is a paradoxical truth that Tantra, a mystical dualism, is more concerned with the concept of Oneness, cosmic unity, than any other religious, mystical, or magical cult. Tantric teachings concerning the nature of time illustrate this concern. In the Western world we *talk* about time as one, referring, for example, to the 'ever-flowing stream of time' as though time was some 'thing' in a state of continuous motion. In practice, however, we atomize time, breaking it into discrete particles labelled 'now' and 'then'. We almost invariably think of our own past lives and the past lives of others—history—as being a series of separate events, sometimes, it is true, connected by a chain of causality but, nevertheless, separate. This occidental interpretation of the nature of time has been compared by Philip Rawson, one of the most perceptive of contemporary commentators on Tantra, with the view seen from the rear window of a speeding car. Objects suddenly appear—that is, events suddenly take place—and recede towards the horizon until they are lost to view. The life of a dead companion is like a slower vehicle which has been passed; we see it in full view from its front to its rear end, and as it recedes, so it seems to get smaller and less significant.

From the point of view of the philosophy of Tantra time is perceived in quite a different way. The past is the *effect* of the present—we, those living at the moment, are conceived of as being, not passengers in the rear seat of a car, but as the mouth of a fire-vomiting dragon. And the past, the dragon's fiery breath, is projected *through* us. Time is a unity; it has no beginning and no end, for past events are projected through each of us. The origin and causes of things are not external to us, for, as Rawson has said, 'their origin is in the projection-mechanism itself . . . within the psycho-physical organism'. An understanding of this—understanding in the sense of interior gnosis, not intellectual comprehension—is the first step towards illumination; or so, at any rate, say the adepts of Tantra.

The tantric conception of the essential unity of time, of past, present, and future as projections of the individual psyche, is merely a special case of a general theory of Oneness. All the opposites of which humanity is conscious can be resolved into a higher unity, the marriage of Shiva and Shakti.

It is not necessary to be a tantric to be instinctively aware that the pairs of opposites of which we are conscious can be transcended, that the duality of existence can be transformed into the unitive life. William James described his own perception of this in *The Varieties of Religious Experience*. He wrote:

Looking back on my own experiences, they all converge towards a kind of insight to which I cannot help ascribing some kind of metaphysical significance. The keynote of it is invariably a reconciliation. It is as if the opposites of the world, whose contradictoriness and conflict make all our difficulties and troubles, were melted into unity. Not only do they, as contrasted species, belong to one and the same genus, but *one of the species*, the nobler and better one, *is itself the genus and so soaks up and absorbs its opposite into itself.* This is a dark saying, I know, when thus expressed in terms of common logic, but I cannot escape from its authority.

Tantrics would tend to see James's belief that one of a particular pair of opposites was 'the nobler and better one' as a cultural prejudice. As far as the philosophy of Tantra is concerned light is neither 'noble' nor 'mean' in comparison with darkness; it is simply different. Both are essential to manifestation, and the same is true of all the pairs of opposites. The entirety of things is a game (*lila*), and the universe we inhabit is 'a *Lila* of the Lady and her Lord', a game played between Shakti and Shiva. The tantric agrees with Bentham that 'poetry is no better than pushpin', but goes much further than the utilitarian.[2] If, says the tantric, the game of pushpin is the polar opposite of poetry, then *poetry could not exist save for the existence of pushpin*. And, of course, vice versa. For the tantric all the opposites are a game of the One, divided for love's sake. In the words of a seventeenth-century mystic: 'For of God and in Him are all things; darkness and light, love and anger, fire and light . . . We live and are in God; we have heaven and hell in ourselves . . .'

The concept of Oneness is implicit in the very word 'Tantra'. For, while the word has etymological connections with other words meaning 'power' and 'beauty', it is generally believed that it is a derivative of a Sanskrit word meaning 'loom'. What is stretched on that loom is a seamless piece of cloth, the totality of things and beings, from atoms to galaxies, from unicellular organisms to men and gods. The warp and the weft, the threads which run the length and breadth of the loom, uniting to form the stretched cloth, are Shiva and Shakti. The analogy is not an exact one, for the warp and weft of a cloth are made up of similar substances, they are both 'form'. Shiva and Shakti are, respectively, form and force—the 'elements' of reality and the dynamic force which interconnects them, sometimes building up, 'creating', sometimes breaking down, 'destroying'. To extend the analogy between the totality of things and a piece of cloth stretched on a loom, Shiva is the form of the cloth, Shakti is the force of tension which binds the individual threads into a *gestalt* in which the whole is greater than the sum of the parts.

The duality of Shakti, her role as *panfagi*, *pangenitor*, 'all-creator, all destroyer', is reminiscent of the god Pan in classical mythology. And, just as Pan was both the gentle Lord of natural things and the destructive Lord of terror, the source of 'panic' in the original sense of the word, so Shakti is both the beautiful and the terrible.

In her kindly aspect she is all the beneficent goddesses of the Hindu pantheon, notably the beautiful Parvati and the self-sacrificing Sati. But she is also Kali, black goddess of death, destruction and murder, and Mother Durga, who brings smallpox as her gift to her children.

---

2. Pushpin was a children's game. Bentham was saying that if poetry provides no greater happiness than a childish game then both, from the point of view of the pleasure-principle, are of equal value.

These love/destruction, life/death, aspects of the power of Shakti are, interestingly enough, mirrored in some of the goddesses of other mythological systems which have never had any contact with either Tantra in particular, nor Indian religion in general. Thus Erzulie, the coquettish Aphrodite of Haitian voodoo, has a violent avatar named Erzulie-ge-Rouge, a red-eyed harridan, filled with hatred and desiring only destruction. Once again it is clear that an aspect of Tantra, in this case a belief that the female Power of the cosmos is characterized by destruction as well as creation, is of worldwide mythological and psychological significance.

The origins of the polarity-philosophy of Tantra are, like the origins of tantric techniques, obscure. But it is significant that there is one profound difference between the underlying concepts expounded in Buddhist tantric texts and that contained in Hindu texts. This difference is not, as might be expected, concerned with the nature of the soul, a tantric recension of the Hindu/Buddhist dispute as to whether there is discrete being at the core of human personality, or whether, as Buddhists believe, there is no more than a bundle of reaction-patterns which humanity labels 'spirit'. The conceptual difference is concerned, rather surprisingly, with the gender of the polarity principles.

As was explained earlier, all devotees of Tantra, whether they be Hindu, Buddhist or Jain, see both the totality of things, the macrocosm of the Western occultist, and the individual human, the microcosm of occultism (a universe-in-miniature) as being made up of pairs of opposites which can, very roughly, be classified as pertaining to either form or force. But while Hindu tantrics see the force-pole, the dynamic element in humanity and the universe which it inhabits, as female (Shakti), and the negative form-pole as male (Shiva), the conception of Buddhist Tantra is exactly reversed. There is what must be described as a gender reversal; for the Buddhist tantric force is male, form is female.

This reversal has, of course, certain practical implications for the tantric who is a Buddhist by religion. It is also possible that it is relevant to the origins of the philosophy of Tantra. The most generally accepted theory is that these origins were exclusively Buddhist and that all varieties of Tantra are ultimately derived from the Vajrayana Buddhism which flourished in the India of a thousand years ago; this theory draws strong support from the fact that the oldest surviving tantric texts are Buddhist, not Hindu.

If Tantra is, indeed, of Buddhist origin, then it is to be presumed that the gender-reversal noted above resulted from a Hindu desire to make Tantra compatible with the 'Great Mother' elements of classical Hinduism. However, the tantric Buddhist concept of the dynamism of the male polarity, the passivity of the female, is at odds with its own religious art. The tantric paintings and sculptures of Tibet and Nepal almost always portray femininity as the active principle. Thus the familiar yab-yum sculptures and icons of Tibet show a god and goddess in ecstatic copulation, with the latter, evidently in vigorous motion, astride the god, who is in a position in which movement would be very difficult, perhaps utterly impossible.

Iconography usually changes more slowly than other aspects of a religion. If such was the case in Tibet, if the religious paintings of the country reflect an earlier stage of tantric Buddhism than do surviving tantric texts, it seems possible that the Hindu version of polarity symbolism antedates the Buddhist.

It is unlikely, however, that Tantra was originally a specifically Hindu movement. Perhaps the most likely possibility is that suggested by Shashibhusan Dasgupta; that all varieties of Tantra derive from an ancient religious cult concerned with sexo-yogic techniques, and that 'Buddhist' and 'Hindu' versions of the cult came into existence as the result of the philosophical speculations of individual practitioners who were influenced by the beliefs of devotees of Buddha, Shakti, and Shiva.

There would be nothing at all surprising if the 'theological' elements discernible in the literature of Tantra were grafted on to the system at some time subsequent to the development of the core techniques, for an astonishingly high proportion of tantric texts are, in a sense, not concerned with Tantra—that is, Tantra as a way of action, a way of liberation. Only some 6 to 7 per cent of tantric literature is directly concerned with mystical techniques involving physical sexuality. The remainder is concerned with such subjects as astrology, the preparation of the symbolic diagrams known as mandalas, and what can only be called 'word magic'—a curious intellectual construct which treats the letters of such languages as Sanskrit as though they were spiritual entities in their own right, capable of acting on their own volition. Some Western students of Tantra, notably 'Arthur Avalon', who managed to combine devotion to Shiva and Shakti with an equally devout Roman Catholicism, have found such word magic to be a worthy subject of study; others have been less impressed.

Whatever the value of word magic, tantric astrology, and similar subjects, there is no doubt that they are no more than a shell which surrounds the kernel of Tantra, i.e. the body of psycho-physical techniques, largely concerned with polarity in general, and human sexuality in particular, which, so it is averred, 'bestow all powers.'

It will seem apparent to some readers of this book that the polarity concepts of Tantra bear at least a passing resemblance to aspects of the variety of qabalistic theory taught in such occult societies as the Golden Dawn, the Stella Matutina, and the 'Rosicrucian Order of the

Alpha et Omega'. Such resemblances are considered at length later, for these analogies and equivalences are, of course, of great interest to the majority of Western occultists.

It would be a pity, however, to totally disregard the analogies between the theoretical structures of Tantra and at least *one* other Western symbol-system than the Golden Dawn version of the qabalah. It seems to me unfortunate that since the publication in the 1930s of Dion Fortune's *Mystical Qabalah* and Israel Regardie's *Garden of Pomegranates* there has been a tendency for English-speaking occultists to disregard non-qabalistic symbol-systems or, at best, to interpret them in exclusively qabalistic terms.

This has resulted in many, perhaps most, contemporary Western occultists being unaware of the very existence of an important element in the Western Esoteric Tradition—the English 'Sophia mysticism' of the seventeenth and eighteenth centuries (briefly referred to in Chapter One) which exerted a formative influence on S. L. MacGregor Mathers and his associates and, through them, on the current renaissance of occultism in general and ritual magic in particular.

The origins of English Sophia mysticism are probably somewhat more complex than is generally thought; those who systematized it seem to have been acquainted with an enormous variety of mystical texts—from the *Works* of Paracelsus to Abiezer Coppe's *Fiery Flying Roll*, from obscure apocalyptic pamphlets produced by members of the 'Family of Love' to the writings of the Christian qabalists. Nevertheless, there is no doubt that the most important single influence on the thought of the English Sophia mystics was the system—if one can so term anything so fluidly dynamic—evolved by the German theosophist Jacob Boehme (1575-1624).

Boehme's writings, most of which were translated into English in the seventeen years between 1645 and 1662, have never been regarded with total approval by orthodox Christians. Thus, in the seventeenth century, Richard Baxter described the reading of Boehme's books as a fit occupation for 'him that hath nothing else to do than to bestow a great deal of time to understand him that was not willing to be easily understood, and to know that his bombasted words do signifie nothing more than before was easily known by common familiar terms'.

There is, of course, a great deal more to Boehme than the expression of old ideas in 'bombasted words', but of his obscurity there can be no doubt, and no two students of Boehme's writings seem to have reached a precise agreement on the meaning of his words. The general structure of Boehme's mystical philosophy, however, seems to be roughly as follows.

The 'primal reality' was God as *der Ungrund*, 'the Abyss', a 'nothing-ness contained everything' which has, in Boehme's own words, 'a longing to reveal itself'. This longing finds expression in a divine introspection in which God 'sees', as in a mirror, the potentialities concealed within Himself.

Boehme identified the Abyss with the first Person of the Trinity, i.e. God the Father, the longing for Self-revelation with God the Son, and the process of 'making' the introspective mirror with God the Holy Spirit. The 'mirror' itself was termed 'Virgin Wisdom', or Sophia, and the wonders God saw 'reflected' in this gave birth to His desire to see these wonders actualized—in other words, to engage in the creative act.

Some supposedly orthodox Christians, for example members of the eighteenth-century Nonjuring Communion led by Dr Deacon of Manchester, have regarded this Behmenist version of Trinitarian doctrine as compatible with historic Christianity. But it is difficult to understand how they could have reasonably adopted this point of view. Quite apart from the fact that the Holy Spirit seems to have been regarded by Boehme as a process, rather than as a Person proceeding from the Father, there seems to be no doubt that the Trinity has been transformed, by some sleight-of-hand of mystical philosophy, into a Quaternary—for the Virgin Wisdom (Sophia) of Boehme is, in some ways, far more of a Person than are either his Son or his Holy Spirit.

Equally incompatible with orthodoxy was Boehme's belief, linked with his concept of Virgin Wisdom, of an 'Eternal Nature', a 'nature' quite distinct from that of matter and time. In his *Open Letter to William Law* John Wesley pointed out that to believe in the existence of this Eternal Nature was to posit the existence of something that was neither created nor Creator—a fatal flaw in Boehme's system from the point of view of Christian theology. In his *Open Letter* Wesley printed an imaginary dialogue which accurately portrayed Law as the mouthpiece of Boehme and himself as the spokesman of orthodox theology:

Law: All that can be conceived is God, or *Nature*, or *Creature*.
Wesley: Is Nature created or not created? It must be one or the other; for there is no Medium. If not created, is it not God? If created, is it not a creature? How then can there be three, God, *Nature* and *Creature*? Since nature must coincide either with God or Creature? . . .
Law: There is an *Eternal Nature*, as universal and *unlimited* as God.

Boehme's 'three principles', which he equated with the Persons of the Trinity, were summarized by Edward Taylor, an Anglo-Irish mystic, as being:

1. The Spring or Fountain of Darkness
2. The Vertue (or Power) of Light
3. The Outbirth out of the Darkness by the power of Light.

The first principle above, the 'Fountain of Darkness', is Boehme's Abyss, *der Ungrund*, the Father; the second, 'the Vertue of Light', is Boehme's 'Son' (the Divine yearning for Self-expression); the third principle is Boehme's Holy Spirit—a process rather than a Person.

Boehme's attribution of the qualities of 'Darkness' and 'Light' to his first and second principle was probably responsible for the form taken by some of the visions of Dr John Pordage (1608-98), one of the most notable of those English mystics who have experienced the embrace of 'Virgin Wisdom'. Both Pordage and his wife experienced what Taylor called 'The Spring or Fountain of Darkness' before they beheld 'The Power of Light'. Pordage described this alarming experience as follows:

We beheld innumerable multitudes of evil spirits . . . presenting themselves in appearing distinctions, of order and dignity . . . there seemed to be inferiority and superiority, Governors and governed. The Princes of this dark world, and their subjects, which presented themselves . . . in state and pomp; all the mighty ones . . . Chariots with six or at least four beasts, to every one, besides every figured similitude of a Coach, was attended with many inferior spirits . . . Those that drew the clowdy Coaches, appearing in the shape of Lions, Dragons, Elephants, Tygers, Bears, and such like terrible beasts; besides the Princes and those that attended them, though all in the shapes of men, yet represented themselves monstrously misshapen, as with ears like those of Cat, cloven feet, ugly legs and bodies, eys fiery, sharp and piercing.

The vision of the 'Power of Light' was, as might be expected, as delightful as the Darkness was terrible. Pordage, his wife, and some associates, beheld:

pure Angelical spirits, in figurative bodies, which were as clear as the morning-star, and transparent as Christal . . . full of Beauty and Majesty . . . sending forth a tincture like the swift rays and hot beams of the Sun, which we powerfully felt to the refreshing of our souls, and enlivening of our bodies . . .

Pordage's visions of the dark and light worlds of Boehme can also be interpreted as a revelation of the cosmic polarity, Shiva and Shakti, seen, as through a glass darkly, through the distorting medium of a mind imbued with the cultural prejudices of a seventeenth-century Protestant. From the point of view of the tantric—and, indeed, from the standpoint adopted in at least some of Boehme's writings—there is nothing intrinsically evil in 'the Fountain of Darkness'; it is just *different*.

This confusion of ethical standards of good and evil with the principle of cosmic polarity runs like a thread through the writings of all the English Sophia mystics—Pordage himself, Richard Roach, Jane Lead, and other, even more obscure, figures who endeavoured to express an inner experience of divine polarity in terms of Protestant theology.

Nevertheless, these writings have a certain value, making it apparent that a personal awareness of, and a direct encounter with, the principle which trantrics term 'Shiva and Shakti' has not been confined to those who, because of their religious environment, have been psychologically predisposed to expect such experiences.

One further point about Pordage which is relevant to polarity-mysticism in general and Tantra in particular is that, throughout his religious life, he was exceptionally strongly influenced—one might almost say dominated—by women. It is true, of course, that women played an important part in all aspects of the religious life of the sixteenth and seventeenth centuries, from the English Missions of the Society of Jesus to the 'Classes' of Anglican Puritanism, but Pordage and his associates were influenced in a much deeper ideological/theological sense. This, in fact, is a characteristic which is pronounced in all varieties of polarity mysticism and, more especially, those in which there is an element of hedonism, of using the senses to overcome the senses.

Why should this be so? On the face of it there seems to be no more reason why men practising hedonistic mysticism, of which Tantra is the most notable variety, should respect women as women, rather than as instruments of pleasure, a means to an end, than they should respect wine as wine, rather than as a pleasurable means to an end. Most, perhaps all, varieties of hedonistic mysticism are concerned with polarity and male devotees aspire towards union with the 'Great Mother', 'Virgin Wisdom', the eternal principle of femininity. They *must* therefore believe that all women are in a sense holy, are particular, rather than general, manifestations of the Great Mother. Women, for a male devotee of hedonistic mysticism, are in a class apart from all other 'instruments' of sensual pleasure—for they are not only the road which the male mystic follows on his journey, they are the goal of his journeying.

CHAPTER THREE
Shiva and the Qabalistic Tree of Life

Since at least the time of Cornelius Agrippa (1486-1535) the qabalah has provided the theoretical basis of most of the practical techniques, both ritual and meditative, employed by Western occultists.

The original qabalah was specifically Jewish. The word is probably derived from an Aramaic Chaldee phrase meaning, very roughly, 'from mouth to ear', so one can safely assume that it was originally an oral tradition, passed from one Rabbinical scholar to another. As with any other oral tradition, it is difficult—perhaps impossible—to know exactly what was the original doctrinal core of the system, but it seems a near certainty that it was concerned with, firstly, a mystical interpretation of the Torah, the first five books of the Old Testament, and, secondly, with a complicated magical/mystical system of word magic rather similar to the tantric system described in the last chapter—although, of course, with the Hebrew rather than the Sanskrit alphabet considered as being sacred emanations of the Primal Voice.

By the fourteenth century most of the oral tradition had assumed a written form, most notably in a vast compilation entitled *Sepher ha-Zohar*, 'the Book of the Splendour'. From this and other qabalist treatises it is clear that at least some qabalists had broken the bonds of Jewish religious rigidity and particularism and were concerned with the same questions of universal significance which have been the preoccupation of the great religious philosophers of all times and all places. If some infinite and totally good power—call it 'God', 'The Absolute', 'Brahma', or any other name—controls the universe, how is the existence of sorrow, suffering, and evil to be explained? Furthermore, if this supreme power, or Being, is limitless, existing independently of any bonds of space and time, how can it be connected in any way with a universe of matter, which not only exists in space and time, but could not possibly exist without them (or, perhaps, vice versa)? Finally, how can humanity, with its puny intellect and limited capacities, in any way experience or know the supreme power?

The answers given by the medieval qabalists bore a strong resemblance to those given by other religious thinkers, East and West, from the Gnostics and Neoplatonists of the late classical world to the Taoist alchemists of China.

The supreme power, it was argued, is *totality*, and, as such contains all aspects of reality, even those which seem contradictory to one another. The Absolute is at one and the same time (or, rather, outside time— eternally) 'good' and 'evil', dark and light, knowable and beyond knowledge or any other comprehension or apprehension. The very interplay of these contradictions is the web of reality; without the eternal opposition and union of the polarized forces—the Yin and Yang of Taoism, the Shiva and Shakti of Tantra—nothing would exist, whether its nature was physical, emotional ('astral'), mental, or spiritual.

As for the nature of the connection between the infinite power and the physical universe of mass, energy, space, and time, this, said the qabalists was to be understood by the use of an optical analogy.

The infinite, unmanifested Power (which the qabalists classified into three different aspects, Ain, Ain Soph, and Ain Soph Aur—'gradations of Unmanifestation', as it were) is like a great Light which shines into a perfect mirror, this mirror being the primal, pure, 'First Manifestation.' This mirror reflects its light into a second mirror, which in turn reflects it into a third mirror, and so on. With each successive reflection the original light source (the unmanifested Absolute) is seen more dimly and distortedly. The final reflection, feeble and warped, is the universe in which mankind lives, moves, and has its being.

The qabalists called these 'mirrors' sephiroth, which is the plural of the Hebrew word sephirah, meaning 'number', and described ten of them. They are as follows:

(I) No.	(II) Hebrew Name	(III) English Translation	(IV) Essential Nature
1	Kether	The Crown	The First Manifestation. The 'pure Absolute' of some philosophers. Existence unqualified by attributes.
2	Chokmah	Wisdom	The 'Ever-Virgin *Sophia*' of some varieties of mysticism. The dynamic cosmic energy. The archetype of which physical sexuality is one expression.

(I) No.	(II) Hebrew Name	(III) English Translation	(IV) Essential Nature
3	Binah	Understanding	The element of stasis. The archetype of form and solidity.
4	Chesed	Mercy	The sphere of organization, of 'concretion of the abstract', the highest level of which the conscious human mind is capable of achieving.
5	Geburah	Severity	Discipline. Order through the use of force. Pure Justice, unassuaged by compassion.
6	Tiphereth	Beauty	The 'place of incarnation', the mysteries of sacrifice.
7	Netzach	Victory	The sphere of artistry, imaginative creation, and the transformation of force. The highest level of 'the astral'.
8	Hod	Glory	The sphere of the 'concrete mind'. A repetition of Chesed on a 'denser' level. Form rather than force. The 'sephirah of ritual magic'.
9	Yesod	The Foundation	The most physical aspect of the astral, the etheric, the sphere of the 'formative forces' of Rudolf Steiner and the anthroposophists.
10	Malkuth	The Kingdom	The physical universe. Solidity, ridigity.

No real significance can be ascribed to the fact that the qabalists described exactly ten sephiroth rather than a greater or lesser number of 'mirrors'. Ten is a convenient number, adequate for the classification of the modes of being, consciousness etc., which are symbolized by the sephiroth, but not so many as to make the system clumsy or even unworkable. Theoretically, however, there is no reason why it should not be considered that a hundred, a thousand, an infinite number of mirrors that reflect the unmanifest Light down towards the material universe.

The system of progressive downwards reflection, through the mirrors of the sephiroth from the Unmanifest to the universe of matter, provides for the qabalist an explanation of how mankind, limited and constrained, can attain to a knowledge of God. Men and women cannot know the infinite-in-itself, but they can transfer their consciousness, their spiritual perception, from the distorted reflection which is Malkuth, the tenth sephirah, the physical universe, to the slightly less distorted reflection of Yesod, the ninth sephirah. And from the ninth to the eighth, and so on.

From the point of view of the contemporary qabalist all the meditative, mystical, and ritual techniques which men have used in order to 'know God', or 'obtain liberation', or 'achieve Nirvana', are methods of transferring consciousness upwards through the successive mirrors of the sephiroth.

As shown in the line drawing on p.53, the qabalists represented the sephiroth in a conventional symbol, called 'the Tree of Life', in which they are shown as ten circles connected by twenty-two 'Paths'. The Paths very approximately indicate some of the interacting influences of the various sephiroth upon one another. It is as though the mirrors reflect in every direction, not just downwards. As an axiom frequently quoted by modern qabalists expresses it, 'Kether is in Malkuth, and Malkuth is in Kether, but after another fashion'.

The Tree of Life is sometimes used as a sort of mental filing system in which the ten sephiroth and the twenty-two Paths are used as gigantic filing cabinets. This arises from the concept that anything whatsoever can be classified in terms of the Tree. Every philosophical, religious, or scientific concept, every myth, legend, and symbol, every aspect of reality from the most densely physical to the most ethereally spiritual can be, so it is held, attributed to one or other of the sephiroth and/or Paths of the Tree.

These attributions, commonly referred to as the correspondences, can be either simple or complex, either grossly obvious or almost deviously subtle. Thus in the simplest way of attributing material objects to the Tree all the physical substance of the manifested universe is attributed to the tenth sephirah, the lowest of the reflecting mirrors. But that tenth sephirah—which, it will be remembered, is called by qabalists Malkuth, 'the Kingdom—can itself be subdivided into ten sephiroth and twenty-two Paths and treated as a Tree of Life itself. This can be done, if one so wishes, with all the sephiroth, individually or collectively—if the latter procedure is followed one ends up, of course, with a hundred sephiroth and two hundred and twenty Paths. This makes for a large and clumsy 'filing system' but, nevertheless, it is sometimes useful in classifying such things as complicated polytheistic systems in terms of the Tree.

Any physical body, animate or inanimate, can be classified in terms of a 'Malkuth Tree' such as that described above. In the case of some parts of the human body, for example, the head would probably be attributed to the first sephirah (Kether, the Crown), the solar plexus would be attributed to the sixth sephirah (Tiphereth, Beauty), the genitals to the ninth sephirah (Yesod, the Foundation), and the feet to perhaps the tenth sephirah (Malkuth, the Kingdom). Such attributions can be fairly flexible and each individual qabalist may adjust them in accordance with his or her own perceptions. Thus in the attribution of the sephiroth to the parts of the human body it might be considered that the anus (dealing as it does with 'the lowest aspects of matter') rather than the feet should be attributed to Malkuth. It is interesting to note, as an illustration of the elasticity of the modes of making attributions to the Tree, that a totally different equation of the human body with the sephiroth can be seen in the illustration entitled 'The Chinese Cosmos' which is printed in Aleister Crowley's *Book of Thoth*.

Ways of attributing the human body to the Tree are of some practical significance, for, as is shown in a later chapter, they enable the Western occultist to, firstly, equate the 'esoteric anatomy' of Tantra with a system with which he or she is more likely to be familiar, and, secondly, to practise a Western modification of the Layayoga employed by many tantric practitioners.

This is not the only way that the qabalistic system of correspondences is relevant to Tantra. As will be subsequently described, they can be applied to the construction of tantric ceremonies which are more effective for most Westerners than would be a slavish adherence to Bengali or Tibetan originals. Before it is possible fully to understand this process it is essential to grasp, at any rate in outline, the way in which systems of qabalistic correspondences have evolved and how they are employed at the present day by practising occultists.

Manuscript and printed lists of the major correspondences between, on the one hand, the thirty-two (ten sephiroth, twenty-two Paths) 'filing cabinets' of the Tree and, on the other hand, such things as colours, numbers, metals, planets, the tarot cards, and the deities of the world's major religions, have been compiled by occultists past and present, from Cornelius Agrippa in the sixteenth century to Major-General J. F. C. Fuller in the 1920s. Of these the most complete is Crowley's 777, first published in 1909 and based on both Golden Dawn manuscripts and Crowley's own researches and intuitions. By their very nature, however, such compilations can never be complete. For, as reality is infinite, a complete list of qabalistic correspondences would have to be of infinite length.

What happens in practice is that each qabalist, having learned by rote some of the major traditional correspondences, creates a personal, ever-growing, correspondence list, classifying everything which is perceived in one to other qabalistic category. At first this is of the nature of task work, calling for much tiresome thought and decision making. Within a very short time, however, the process becomes completely automatic, calling for no conscious effort.

Some of the traditional correspondences are seemingly arbitrary, but there is usually a psychological, archetypal rationale which explains them. Before giving an example of such a rationale it is perhaps worth saying that complex chains of correspondence, such as that very briefly outlined below, were not part of the 'original qabalah' expounded by medieval Jewish rabbis. They are probably no more than five hundred or so years old—the qabalah, like Tantra, is a living system, in process of continual evolution. Nevertheless, the use of chains of correspondences is not only to be discerned in the writings of such medieval Jewish scholars as Maimonides but is perfectly compatible with the earliest surviving qabalistic texts.

Some of the traditional attributions of the fifth sephirah, Geburah, provide a good example of a correspondence chain. These attributions include all war gods, the planet Mars, the plant *nux vomica*, various shades of the colour red, the horse, and iron. What possible relationship can there be between the various items of this extraordinary collection?

To answer this question one must first remember that Geburah, the fifth sephirah, is the symbol of the destructive element of manifested reality. It is immediately apparent that all gods of war and destruction must be attributed to this sephirah.

The relationship with the planet Mars is almost equally obvious, quite apart from the fact that its name is identical with that of the Roman god of war. In astrology Mars has always been seen as the planet which, in the horoscopes of both individuals and nations, signifies belligerence, war, murder, and sudden violent death. Therefore the person whose horoscope is dominated by a pattern of planetary aspects dominated by Mars is supposedly likely to be the possessor of an aggressive and even violent personality.

Perhaps the most interesting attributions are those of the various shades of the colour red. Even to the naked eye the light reflected to Earth from Mars has a faintly reddish tinge; red is the colour of blood, and thus of bloodshed and the tumults and wars which are productive of it; red is traditionally associated with violent energy and even with life itself—probably this was the origin of the primitive custom of staining red the bones of the tribe's honoured dead. Such staining was usually carried out with haematite and other naturally occurring ferrous compounds. This provides one reason why iron is attributed to Geburah. Another is that iron became the sacred metal of many war gods after it had displaced bronze as the usual material from which swords, spears, and other edged weapons were manufactured. Still another is that there may be some measurable physical influence exerted on the metal iron by the planet Mars. This, of course, would seem inherently improbable, but a series of experiments undertaken by a number of anthroposophical scientists, notably the late Dr Lili Kolisko, would seem to show that the traditional qabalistic correspondences between metals and particular planets—Mars and iron, Jupiter and tin, and so on—have a physical basis.

The oddest element in the qabalistic correspondence chain associated with Geburah is the horse; after all, even a stallion is a fairly placid animal compared with, say, a Siberian white tiger or a bull elephant. In part the association may be arbitrary, based on the fact that in ancient Greece the horse was held to be peculiarly sacred to Ares, god of war. It is worth noting, however, that the first people to use iron weapons in warfare seem to have been the ancient Hittites, who were also the first warriors to go into battle in horse-drawn chariots. Perhaps that is why the horse is one of the animals sacred to Geburah.

Save for the possible physical connection between the metal iron and the planet Mars, none of the above connections are 'logical' in a scientific sense. That is, there is no rigid cause-and-effect relationship between, say, horses and nux vomica. Nevertheless, on a psychological level the correspondences are very real indeed, and, used in the course of occult rites and ceremonies they seem to be effective as aids to the establishment of a relationship with what are sometimes called 'the hidden forces of nature.'

This is done as follows. If an occultist wishes to achieve a result compatible with the nature of Geburah—for example 'a work of destruction'—he constructs a magical ceremony on the basis of the correspondences associated with that sephirah. He will, for example, wear red garments, stand in a five-pointed star drawn in red chalk inside a pentagon, carry an iron sword, and chant verses associated with the gods of war. If he has an altar he will cover it with a five-sided cloth, and on it will stand a censer in which smoulder substances traditionally associated with Mars and other war gods. Those familiar with Aleister Crowley's novel Moonchild, which contains much magical and qabalistic lore under the guise of fiction, will remember that it contains a description of just such a 'work of destruction.' The ceremony described involves a tarot card, numbered XVI and named 'The Blasted Tower', being placed upon the altar. At first sight this seems strange, for, as shown by reference to such a printed list of correspondences as Crowley's 777, this card is not attributed to any of the sephiroth, but to a Path. The explanation of how a tarot card corresponding to a Path be used in an occult working pertaining to a sephirah provides a good example of the complexity and versatility of the qabalistic Tree of Life.

As was previously explained, the planet Mars is one of the correspondences of Geburah, the fifth sephirah. But the same planet also corresponds, particularly in its subjective astrological significance as the destructive, energetic aspect of the human psyche, to the seventeenth Path of the qabalistic Tree of Life. This means that there is a continual interplay of subtle energies and influences between the powers of the seventeenth Path, to which the tarot card numberd XVI is attributed, and those of the fifth sephirah, Geburah. This card, 'The Blasted Tower', could therefore be very suitably employed in a working under the rulership of Geburah.

In due course it will be described how the correspondences of the Tree of Life, particularly those relating to Binah, the third sephirah, and Chokmah, the second Sephirah, can be applied to tantric workings. First, however, it must be considered how far one can relate the theoretical and philosophical concepts associated with Tantra to the seemingly similar concepts associated with the qabalah and symbolically expressed in the Tree of Life.

Tantra sees all manifestation as an aspect of the fundamental polarities of Shiva and Shakti, form and force, static and dynamic, male and female; in other words, all existence is a by-product of the eternal love-play between the polarities. A curiously similar concept can be discerned in certain medieval and renaissance qabalistic texts dealing with what is called 'Shekinah'.

A problem in defining any mystical or magical terms is that each writer or speaker seems to have his or her own personal interpretation of its meaning. Thus, for example, such familiar occult terms as 'etheric', 'astral', and 'psychic', have no fixed meaning, and a type of out-of-the-body experience referred to by one occult authority as 'astral projection' will be referred to by another as 'etheric projection'. The problem is particularly acute with the terms used in qabalism and the Merkabah ('Chariot') mysticism which so profoundly influenced it. The word Shekinah provides a good example of this. It has sometimes been used as though it meant no more than a synonym for the tenth sephirah, Malkuth. Sometimes it has also been used in this way but with the name Malkuth being given a totally different significance from that customary in the qabalism of contemporary occultists. On other occasions the term Shekinah has been used in very much the same sense as that in which a Christian theologian uses the term Holy Spirit. It is also sometimes used as though it was the name of the 'Platonic idea' of the community of Israel—Israel as it *should* be, Israel as it *would* have been but for the Fall of Man, Israel as it *will* be after the Messiah has redeemed it.

It is in the last sense that the concept of the Shekinah can be most clearly seen in relation to Tantra. The Unmanifest (Ain Soph, Ain, Ain Soph Aur), 'the Innermost Being of God', is the Bridegroom of Shekinah, 'the Queen', and their offspring are the sephiroth and the Paths—the totality of manifestation. The analogies between this and the Shiva-Shakti teachings of Tantra are apparent.

Curiously enough, few of the occult qabalists of the present century—Dion Fortune, Israel Regardie, Aleister Crowley, etc.—have shown much interest in Shekinah concepts. Some of them, indeed, seem hardly to have been aware of the existence of them. It is worthy of remark, however, that while no written teachings concerning the Shekinah were circulated amongst the initiates of the Golden Dawn, the concept of Malkuth as the Shekinah, the Bride of God, is implicit in certain diagrams on which members of the so-called Portal Grade were instructed to engage in prolonged meditation.

The diagrams in question are concerned with the Fall—that devastating event in humanity's psychic evolution which is recounted in Genesis under the allegorical form of a study concerning Adam, Eve, and the forbidden fruit which the serpent persuaded them to eat.

The first of these diagrams, known as 'The Garden of Eden Before the Fall', was placed upon the cubical altar in a Golden Dawn temple during an initiation to the occult grade of Practicus. Amongst other things it showed — to quote the ritual in question—'the great ADAM, the Son who was to Rule the Nations with a Rod of Iron . . . and in Malkuth is EVE, Mother of All, the Completion of All, and above the Universe she supporteth with her hands the Eternal Pillars of the Sephiroth. As it was said to you *Above the shoulders* of that Great Goddess is Nature in her vastness exalted.'

The second of these diagrams. 'The Garden of Eden after the Fall', showed a shattered Tree of Life. This shattering was explained in the Golden Dawn's ritual for the occult grade of Philosophus as being the result of 'The Great Goddess Eve' being tempted by the fruit of the Tree of Knowledge.

There are many points of interest about these brief extracts from the rituals of the Golden Dawn. Firstly, the 'Great Goddess Eve' is specifically stated to have supported 'Nature' upon her shoulders before the Fall. It is apparent that this 'Nature' is not the 'nature' of books devoted to ecology, but the Eternal Nature of Jacob Boehme and his disciples. Secondly, implicit in these passages is the idea that Eve is the Shekinah, the Bride, an everlasting principle whose relationship with another Eternal has given rise to the sephiroth—the worlds of manifestation as we know them. Finally, it would seem clear that this 'Great Goddess Eve' is one and the same as the 'Eternal Eve', the Ever Virgin *Sophia*, with whom, as was explained earlier, the hedonist mystic Eva von Buttlar identified herself.

It is now obvious that the Shiva-Shakti polarity of Tantra can be equated with qabalism by identifying Malkuth, as the Shekinah, with one of the tantric polarities, and the Unmanifest with the other.

In either case there will, of course, be a gender-reversal of the type described in relation to Buddhist tantrism. That is to say, the female Shakti principle—the active, dynamic, force-pole of Tantra—must be identified with the masculine force-pole (either the Unmanifest or the first three sephiroth) of qabalism. Similarly, the male principle (Shiva), the passive form-pole of Tantra, must be equated with the female Shekinah, the qabalistic form-pole.

While the approach outlined above provides a reasonably satisfactory theoretical reconciliation between the Tantra of Bengal and the qabalah of the Western occultists, it is not particularly useful in practical terms— i.e. it is difficult to see how it could be used in either ritual workings or in the sort of meditative work, using symbols as an aid to the creative imagination, which is commonly employed by Western esotericists. For, by definition, the only symbol which can express the Unmanifest is nothing—a difficult thing to think about and an even more difficult one to employ as an implement in an occult working on the physical plane.

Fortunately, the qabalistic Tree of Life is a symbol which can be quite legitimately employed in many different ways. Thus, for example, most occult qabalists of the last and the present century have considered the sephirah Tiphereth to be the 'Christ centre' of the Tree of Life, and have sought to understand the significance of sacrifice in general, and divine sacrifice in particular, by considering Tiphereth in relationship to the other sephiroth of the Tree. This approach has been productive, no doubt, of many useful insights—but it is by no means the only possible approach. In the seventeenth century the occultist John Heyden, a self-styled Rosicrucian whose writings exerted a strong influence upon S. L. MacGregor Mathers and his associates,[1] regarded

---

1. Thus, as pointed out by Stephen Skinner in his book *Terrestrial Astrology* (Routledge), the Golden Dawn instructions for the practice of geomancy, which involved the use of the sigils of spirits — a use not found in standard geomantic systems — was almost certainly derived from Heyden.

Chokmah, the second sephirah, as being the Christ centre, and Binah, the third sephirah, as being peculiarly associated with the Holy Spirit. In his *Harmony of the World* (1662) he wrote: 'the second light, is called *Jod Tetragrammaton*, and he is attributed to the second person, *Jesus Christ*, and at his command *Hochma* [Chokmah] . . . The third light is called *Elohim Jehovah*, and is attributed to the *Holy Ghost*, he commands *Binah* . . '

Some qabalists have attributed Christ to no particular sephirah, and in his *Mosaicall Philosophy* the writer Robert Fludd identified the Messiah with the Tree of Life as a whole, with Kether, which he called 'the fountain and root of infinity', as the link between the Father and the Son.

Using the same sort of versatile approach as that employed by Heyden and Fludd it would be possible to attribute *any* pair of sephiroth to the Shiva-Shakti polarities of Tantra. But the most suitable would undoubtedly be the same sephiroth to which John Heyden attributed the second and third Persons of the Holy Trinity, namely Chokmah and Binah, the second and third sephiroth of the Tree of Life. In the table printed on page 39 it will be seen that I have described the 'Essential Nature' of Chokmah as the '. . *Sophia* of some varieties of mysticism. The dynamic cosmic energy. The archetype of which physical sexuality is one expression.' In the same table Binah is described as being 'The element of stasis. The archetype of form and solidity.'

The relevance of these descriptions to an identification of Chokmah with Shakti, and Binah with Shiva, is clear—although it would perhaps be best if the phrase 'The archetype of physical sexuality . . ' was applied, not directly to Chokmah itself, but to the relationship *between* Chokmah and Binah, force and form.

If the equation between Shiva/Shakti and Chokmah/Binah is one that can legitimately be made—and the evidence that this is so is very strong indeed—then the Western occultist can learn a great deal about the fundamental natures of the great polarities of Tantra in terms of symbol-systems with which he is more familiar.

The occult qabalah of the Golden Dawn and other, less well known, groups who were numbered amongst both the forerunners and successors of that fraternity, is the supreme example of such a symbol-system. But it is by no means the only system which is relevant to this enquiry. Others include alchemy, the somewhat scholastic and 'qabalized' version of Behmenist mysticism which was current in the England of the Commonwealth and the Restoration, and even Western astrology and geomancy.

It is best to concentrate, however, on a consideration of the concepts of Chokmah and Binah as they are described in the writings of the occult qabalists. These concepts are, of course, by no means identical with the teachings of the rabbinical qabalists of the Middle Ages; as has been said before, the qabalah is a system which is still in process of change and evolution. From the point of view of pure scholarship such change can be regarded as being (as one commentator has described it) 'a process of syncretistic degeneration'. From the point of view of the practising occultist, however, any system which is rigidly ossified is of little practical utility, because it can never cope with the demands made upon it by new conditions—changes in the physical, intellectual, and ethical environments of humanity. It must therefore be held in mind that the descriptions of Chokmah/Binah given below will show marked variations from the way in which those sephiroth would have been described by a Lurianic qabalist of the sixteenth century, and even more divergence from the way in which they would have been regarded by a fourteenth-century disciple of Moses de Leon, the compiler of the *Sepher ha-Zohar*.

Strictly speaking, one should not consider the Chokmah/Binah sephiroth except in relationship to the other eight sephiroth and the Paths which interconnect them. In practice, however, one can get a very good idea of the Chokmah/Binah polarity without having to make reference to those seven sephiroth, from Chesed to Malkuth, which are numbered 4-10 on the Tree (see line drawing on page 53). But it is impossible to examine Chokmah and Binah in total isolation from Kether, the first 'crystallization' from the Unmanifest; the triad of Kether-Binah-Chokmah, the 'supernal sephiroth', are so interconnected with one another that some Christian qabalists, such as John Heyden quoted earlier, have gone so far as to identify them with the three Persons of the Nicene and other Christian Creeds.

In what is sometimes referred to by contemporary qabalists as 'the Yetziratic texts'—a collection of somewhat gnomic statements about the sephiroth and Paths which was first printed in the sixteenth century and probably dates from only a little earlier [2] —Kether is described as:

the admirable or hidden intelligence because it is the light giving the power of comprehension of the first principle, which hath no beginning. And it is the primal glory, because no created being can attain to its essence.

This statement is somewhat less obscure than many other of the Yetziratic texts; like all of them, however, it seems to contain an element of paradox. On the one hand Kether is described as giving the power of comprehending the first principle, which it must be presumed means

---

2. These 'Yetziratic texts' are not *part* of the ancient *Sepher Yetzirah*, the qabalistic *Book of Formation*; they are simply printed as an appendix to most editions of that work.

the Unmanifest, God in His hiddenness. But on the other hand it is specifically stated that it is impossible to 'attain to its essence'. On the face of it, then, the text states that Kether gives something which no created being can possibly receive. What was originally intended to be communicated by this statement can be surmised but not known.

However, what some qabalists of modern times have interpreted it to mean is as follows. Kether, the first concretion or 'densification' of the Unmanifest, may be regarded as 'form' in comparison with the Unmanifest, but from the point of view of any creature—i.e. any created being, from an archangel to an amoeba—it is pure 'force' and, consequently, its essence by definition unattainable. However, it is possible, so it is argued, for a created being to temporarily or permanently cease, in effect, to be a creature—to become 'pure energy' and attain to the essence of Kether, thus becoming capable of comprehending the Unmanifest.

This hypothetical 'attainment to the essence of Kether' is held to be identical with the Divine Union of the mystics. Few qabalists have claimed to have experienced such a Union—as the late Israel Regardie remarked, to make such a claim sets a giant question mark against its validity—but, nevertheless, some modern occult qabalists have written interestingly of the 'attainment of Kether'. Notable amongst these was Dion Fortune, who in her *Mystical Qabalah* (Williams and Norgate, 1935) asserted that the experience was incompatible with the survival of 'the vehicle of incarnation', by which she meant not only the physical body and the underlying formative forces associated with it, but that 'vehicle of consciousness' which Paracelsus called the astral body. Those who have 'attained Kether', she said, 'are the prototypes of those supermen concerning whom all races have a tradition'. In other words, they are those to whom the followers of H. P. Blavatsky refer as 'the Masters'.

In terms of Tantra, those who have attained to Kether are, quite simply, those who are in a state of consciousness where the Shiva/Shakti polarity no longer exists—or, to be more precise, where that polarity only exists when the adept *wants* it to exist.

It is perhaps a mistake for the occult student to spend too much time trying to define the precise nature of the supreme mystical experience, whether one chooses to label that experience as 'Kether attainment', 'tantric adepthood', or even nirvana. The nature of an ineffable experience is, by definition, incommunicable and incapable of apprehension save through personal experience. It is worth remembering that the 'magical image' of Kether (i.e. the picture-image an occult qabalist uses to represent that sephirah) is 'an ancient bearded King seen in profile'. This image has usually been represented as no

more than a symbolic way of expressing the concept of Kether as a
bridge between the manifest universe on one side, and the Unmanifest
on the other. But it also conveys the idea that created beings get a
(literally) one-sided view of the state of consciousness which is
symbolized, on the Tree of Life, by Kether.

Even our one-sided view of Kether can only be properly achieved
when we cease to try to look at it in isolation and consider it as one
of the component elements of the supernal triangle of Kether-Chokmah-
Binah; in this connection it is worth remembering some words attributed
to 'the Master Koot Hoomi' by Madame Blavatsky, founder of the
Theosophical Society. 'There can be no manifestation', Koot Hoomi
is alleged to have said, 'without differentiation into pairs of opposites.'
Whether Koot Hoomi actually said these words—indeed, whether Koot
Hoomi enjoyed any objective existence outside Madame Blavatsky's
fertile imagination—is of no great moment. For there can be no doubt
that the sentiment, whoever first expressed it, is good qabalism—and
good Tantra. For Kether (and its tantric equivalent, non-polarity) is
not, as far as the physical universe is concerned, existence, but the
forerunner of existence. The same principle is true in relationship to
human psychology; Kether is not consciousness, but the 'energy stuff'
from which consciousness emerges.

Such 'rational' arguments for considering the three supernals in
relationship to one another, rather than in isolation, are supported
by the very ancient qabalistic technique of attributing the ten sephiroth
to 'Seven Palaces'. In the first of these are placed Kether, Chokmah,
and Binah; the next five 'Palaces' are occupied by one each of the
sephiroth from Chesed to Netzach inclusive; the seventh is occupied
by Yesod and Malkuth.

Chokmah, Wisdom, is sometimes referred to by qabalists as Abba,
'the Supernal Father', while Binah is given the title of Ama, 'the Supernal
Mother'. In other words, Kether, the 'raw material' of manifestation
and consciousness, is differentiated into the active, dynamic, potency
of Chokmah, and the static, passive potency of Binah.

The qabalah originated in a cultural environment in which
physiological maleness in its most physical sense, i.e. the possession of
testicles, was seen as a manifestation of the ultimate dynamic principle,
while physiological feminity was seen as a manifestation of the primal
principle of negativity and stasis. As a consequence of this cultural
factor, which is in no way an indication of underlying philosophical
divergence between qabalism and Tantra, Chokmah and Binah have
a gender-inversion, a polarity reversal, from the point of view of anyone
who conceptualizes the cosmic duality in terms of the Tantra of Bengal

and other parts of India. It is therefore apparent that it is a considerable over-simplification to identify without qualification—as is done in that compilation of qabalistic correspondences known as 777—Chokmah with Shiva and Binah with Shakti. For, although Tantra and the qabalah are in agreement that the positive, dynamic, aspect of manifestation was the eldest 'child' of primal non-duality, the tantrics of India consider the active principle to be female while the qabalists (like, it will be remembered, Buddhist tantrics) regard it as male.

It would therefore seem clear that it could be misleading to make a simple equation of Chokmah, the Supernal Father of the qabalists, with Shiva, the male principle of Tantra. It would, of course, be similarly misleading to regard Binah, the Supernal Mother of the qabalists, as being absolutely identical with Shakti.

It could be argued that a concern with the exact nature of the equivalence between the Chokmah/Binah polarity and the Shiva/Shakti polarity savours of scholastic hair-splitting and, as such, can be safely thought of as being irrelevant to the essentially practical concerns of Tantra, the Way of Action.

This, however, is not necessarily the case. For the gender reversal between tantric and qabalistic concepts of polarity may have important implications for some Western occultists; those who wish to engage in tantric meditations or rituals which are expressed in a symbol-system consonant with the Western Esoteric Tradition—that synthesis of occult theory and technique which is particularly associated with the Golden Dawn and its derivatives.

It seems likely that Western occultists experimenting with Tantra may experience considerable difficulties if they attempt to apply *all* the concepts, correspondences, etc., associated with Binah, the Great Mother of the qabalistic Tree of Life, to Shakti, the Great Mother of Indian Tantra. Very much the same sort of problems might be encountered in applying all Chokmah symbolism to Shiva.

It is clear that problems of this nature cannot be satisfactorily overcome by the device of simple reversal, e.g. applying the concepts/symbols of the qabalistic Mother to the Shiva of Tantra. For while *some* Binah concepts may refer to Shiva, not Shakti, others quite clearly refer to Shakti, the Great Mother of all manifestation. With Chokmah the opposite situation prevails. Some of the major correspondences and attributions employed by contemporary occultists in relation to Chokmah and Binah are as outlined below. In considering the various elements of these lists it must be remembered that while such attributions are collectively described as being 'traditional' some of them are of comparatively recent origin:

Name of Sephirah	Chokmah (Wisdom)	Binah (Understanding)
Astrological Correspondence	The Zodiac	Saturn
Elemental Attribution	Root of Fire	Root of Water
Colours	Soft Blue, Grey, Mother of Pearl, White flecked with Red, Blue and Yellow	Crimson, Black, Dark Brown, Grey flecked with Pink
Egyptian gods	Nuit (as zodiac), Isis in her Wisdom aspect	Isis, Nephthys
Hindu 'gods'	Akasa (as form)	Prana (as force)
Buddhist Meditation	Joy	Compassion
Animals	All Males	All Females
Plants	Amaranth, Mistletoe	Cypress, Poppy, Lotus, Lily
Stones	Turquoise	Pearl
Perfumes	Musk	Myrrh, Civet
Geometrical Figures	The Cross	The Triangle
Alchemical Element	Sulphur	Salt

If one is to equate Chokmah with Shiva as the negative, static pole of the cosmic opposition, and Binah with Shakti, the positive dynamic pole, these correspondences are inadequate and misleading.

Firstly, the astrological correspondences must be reversed; Shakti corresponds with the moving dynamism astrologically attributed to the zodiac, not with Saturnian qualities of solidity and stability.

The elemental attribution is also unsatisfactory. Clearly, as the Great Mother, Shakti has a water aspect—the sea, after all, is the source of all life on this planet. Shakti also has, as will be explained in the next chapter, aspects pertaining to earth. But the essential quality of Shakti is its dynamism, which pertains to what the ancients called 'elemental Fire.'

The colours shown in the above table would probably be effective in a tantric working, but it would undoubtedly be simpler to use one of the many tantric colour schemes traditionally associated with the Shiva/Shakti polarity—violet for Shiva and orange-red for Shakti, for example.

The reader should be able to work out other sensible adjustments to the table printed above. Thus, for example, it will be obvious that Nuit, the Egyptian star-goddess, pertains to Shakti rather than Shiva, and that the alchemical principle of sulphur—i.e. motion, change—equates with Shakti rather than Shiva.

The necessity for such adjustments makes it apparent that while qabalism can be harmonized with Tantra there can be no easy, semi-automatic equation between the two.

As will be shown in the next two chapters, the same is true of the systems of esoteric physiology associated with Tantra, on the one hand, and qabalism on the other.

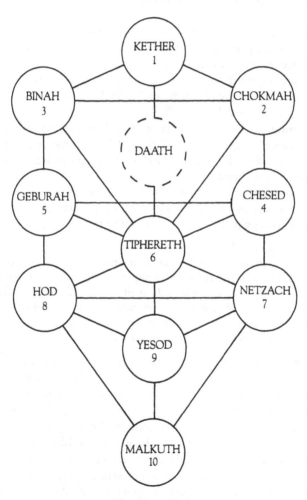

The Tree of Life

CHAPTER FOUR
Esoteric Physiology

The experience of the cosmic duality of Shiva and Shakti can be overwhelming, particularly for the psychologically unprepared. Some who have undergone it have become, for a time, speechless. Others have misinterpreted the experience. Thus, as was mentioned earlier, the English Sophia mystics, such as John Pordage, perceived the negative aspect of polarity as being 'evil.'

Sometimes such misinterpretations have been crudely physical, and some material object has had all the qualities of one or other of the polarities attributed to it in a manner which contradicts all the laws of physics and chemistry.

It is possible that some such subjective misinterpretation of an inner experience was responsible for some of the more eccentric expressions of opinion contained in the writings of D. H. Lawrence. For example:

The sun is polarized with the solar plexus in mankind . . . the sun is the great fiery vivifying pole of the inanimate universe, the moon is the other pole, cold and keen and vivifying, corresponding in some way to a *voluntary* pole. We live between the polarized circuit of sun and moon . . . Sun and Moon are dynamically polarized to our actual tissue, they affect this tissue all the time . . . Light and dark, these great wonders, are relative to us alone. These are two vast poles of the cosmic energy.

It seems to me that the above passage, even when due consideration is given to the fact that Lawrence enjoyed shocking and alarming his contemporaries, is far more than an expression, serious or tongue-in-cheek, of unlikely astronomical theories. The probability is that Lawrence had undergone some personal revelation—perhaps coinciding with his reading of books by C. G. Jung and H. P. Blavatsky—and had experienced a vision of, or an illumination concerning, the Shiva/Shakti polarity. This he later endeavoured to express in quasi-astronomical language, attributing the dynamic qualities of Shakti to the sun, and the static qualities of Shiva to the moon.

It is interesting to note that *Fantasia of the Unconscious* (1923), the book from which the above passage is quoted, contains numerous unsubstantiated statements about various supposed psychic functions of the solar plexus, the lumbar ganglion, and the cardiac plexus. It may well be that statements of this type were no more than Lawrentian derivations of theories he had become acquainted with through reading Theosophical books and pamphlets. But there seems to be some possibility that he had arrived, perhaps as the result of an inner experience, at a muddled, but genuinely intuitive, understanding of the system of esoteric physiology which is particularly associated with Tantra and the Layayoga of Bengal and other parts of India. For the supposed human psychic centres ('chakras', or 'wheels') of the esoteric physiology of Tantra are believed to be closely associated with, although not identical to, at least some of the physical organs which Lawrence regarded as being concerned with his hypothetical sun/moon polarity.

At the centre of Tantra's physiological teachings is the concept, mentioned earlier in this book and familiar to students of Western occultism, of man as a microcosm, a 'universe in miniature' which reflects every aspect of the macrocosm, 'the great universe'. The macrocosm is, it must be remembered, the totality of things; not just the physical universe of galaxies, stars, and planets, existing in space-time, but the universe of gods, angels, demons, spiritual, and astral beings. Everything—and every mode of being which is part of the totality is included in each and every individual human being. As one tantric text puts it: 'He who realizes the truth of the body can come to know the truth of the universe'; in other words, the human body is an expression of the same Shiva/Shakti polarity which manifests itself as the totality, the macrocosm, and by journeying into 'inner space' the individual can attain to a knowledge, an authentic gnosis, of the totality.

Through the five senses of smell, taste, sight, hearing, and touch the individual relates to the macrocosm as a physical entity, i.e. to the world of matter and to those energies, such as light and electro-magnetism, which can be directly or indirectly observed through the senses. These senses, however, cannot perceive all aspects of reality; the physical body as such is unable to apprehend those modes of being which are referred to as astral or spiritual in the terminology of Western occultism.

As far as the tantric is concerned the points of contact between the individual on the one hand, and non-physical energies and beings on the other, are the chakras, psychic energy centres which are associated with particular areas of the body, but are not *part* of the body.

There is no agreement on the exact number of energy centres existing in each human being. Several tantric texts asserted that there are no less than 88,000 of them; mercifully, they neither name them nor list their functions and attributes. Generally it is agreed that there are some thirty major chakras, some of them situated in such unlikely places as the tip of the nose, all of them interconnected by subtle energy channels, the psychic equivalents of nerves, arteries, and veins, which are called nadis. Seven of the chakras are of the greatest importance in the tantric system of esoteric physiology. These are:

1. The *Muladhara chakra*, associated with (not situated in) the perineum, the area between the genitals and the anus.

2. The *Svadisthana chakra*, associated with the area immediately above the genitals, more or less the *mons veneris*.

3. The *Manipura chakra*, associated with the epigastric (i.e. solar) plexus—the plexus to which D. H. Lawrence attached so much importance.

4. The *Anahata chakra*, associated with the cardiac plexus, another psychic centre in which Lawrence displayed particular interest.

5. The *Vishuddha chakra*, associated with the area of the body in which the larynx and pharynx are situated.

6. The *Ajna chakra*, associated with an area of the body commencing between the eyebrows and extending roughly halfway down the nose.

7. The *Sahasrara chakra*, associated with a subtle extension of the physical body which is supposedly above the crown of the head.

The first of these chakras, the Muladhara, which name means something very roughly equivalent to the English word foundation, is of particular interest to the student of Tantra. For, as was briefly explained earlier, it is supposedly the dwelling place of the mysterious Kundalini, symbolically conceived of as a sleeping serpent, the latent power of Shakti, which lies coiled—one meaning of the word Kundalini is 'the coiled one'—and awaiting arousal.

Kundalini is visualized as the very core of the Muladhara chakra, it being enclosed within a triangle with its base pointing downwards, a very obvious symbol of female sexuality, which is itself situated within a yellow square, symbolic of the 'element' of Earth. Many Western occultists will be familiar with the symbolism of this yellow square, which, over a century ago, was harmonized with the Western Esoteric Tradition by S. L. MacGregor Mathers and those associated with him in the Hermetic Order of the Golden Dawn.

In a later chapter the way in which aspects of the tantric tradition have been absorbed into Western occultism will be described in some detail. At this stage it suffices to give a description of how certain geometric symbols, each associated with a particular charm, are used by Western occultists as a means of inducing clairvoyant visions and 'astral projection.'

The basic technique, still in use at the present day, is described in various Golden Dawn instructional documents which are collectively known as the Flying Rolls. The experimenter is first instructed to make a set of 'tattva cards'—tattvas are coloured geometric symbols, derived from the symbolism of the chakras.[1] There are five 'primary tattvas'. They are:

1. A yellow square, known as Prithivi, associated, as was mentioned above, with the qualities symbolized as 'elemental Earth' and the Muladhara chakra.

2. A silver-white crescent moon, lying on its back with its horns pointing upwards, known as Apas. This symbol is particularly associated with 'elemental Water', with certain aspects of female sexuality, and with the Svadisthana chakra. It will be remembered that this chakra is closely related to the area of the body situated immediately above the genitals.

3. A red-tinged-with-orange, equilateral triangle, its apex pointing upwards, known as Tejas. Its shape is identical with that of the symbol used by Western alchemists to indicate the fiery energies of nature. This is in conformity with its tantric significance as the symbol of 'elemental Fire' and its association with the Manipura chakra—a psychic analogue of the solar plexus.

4. A sky-blue circle (bluish white, according to some tantric texts, which describe it as resembling 'the full moon in blueness') known as Vayu, and symbolizing 'elemental Air'. At least some tantric texts associate this tattva with the Vishuddha chakra, a psychic analogue of the throat roughly corresponding to the pharynx and larynx.

5. An irregular elliptic figure, somewhat in the shape of an egg, and named Akas. Strictly speaking it should be colourless, representing the immateriality of Akas, 'elemental Spirit'. In practice it is usually coloured a dark blue, almost approaching indigo. It is thought to symbolize, amongst many other things, the Ajna chakra, which is sometimes thought of as being a gateway between matter and the worlds of spirit. This chakra, as stated earlier, is associated with

---

1. As will be seen from some subsequent quotations, 'tattwa', rather than 'tattva', was the form of English transliteration most usually employed by initiates of the Golden Dawn.

the area between the eyebrows; it is also held to have a particular relationship with the 'third eye', i.e. the pineal gland.

From the five primary tattvas are derived twenty composite sub-tattvas, which are represented by the display of a miniature version of any one of the prime tattvas on a delineation of any one of the others. This sounds complex, but in practice it is very simple. Thus, for example, a miniature red equilateral triangle mounted on a larger yellow square would be referred to as 'Tejas of Prithivi' and would represent 'Fire of Earth', the Fiery aspects of dense matter—or, to put it in the terms of tantric esoteric physiology, the more fiery elements in the Muladhara chakra where the serpent power lies sleeping, the glowing spark at the heart of the sleeping Kundalini.

If the situation was reversed (that is, if a miniature yellow square was mounted on a red equilateral triangle), what was represented would be Prithvi of Tejas, 'Earth of Fire', the weightier aspects of those qualities in nature and humanity which are described as being 'fiery'.

One way in which the tattvas are, and have been, used by Western occultists, is described in a Golden Dawn document, Flying Roll XXXVI, which was written by Moina Mathers, sister of the philosopher Henri Bergson and wife of S. L. MacGregor Mathers. She wrote:

Take the tattwa cards and choose one at random, without looking to see what symbol it may represent, and lay it on a table face downwards. Then try mentally to discover the symbol. To do this make your mind a blank as much as possible (yet always keeping control over the same) chasing therefrom, for the time being, the power of reason, memory etc. You will find that after a few moments of gazing attentively at the back of the card, that it will seem as though the thought form of the tattwa appeared to enter the mind suddenly, and later, when more practised, it will probably appear to you as if the tattwa symbol were trying to precipitate itself materially through the back of the card.

Supposing the symbol you were experimenting with was Prithivi of Apas, that is, the 'earthly aspect of elemental Water', represented by a miniature yellow square mounted on a silver crescent, then fill your mind with the ideas thus symbolized. Place the tattwa card before you . . . and look at the symbol long and steadily until you can perceive it clearly as a thought vision when you shut your eyes . . . It may help you to perceive it as a large crescent made of blue or silvery water containing a cube of yellow sand. Continue trying to acquire a keen perception of the tattwa until . . . its shape and its qualities shall seem to have become a part of you, and you should then begin to feel as though you were one with that particular Element, i.e. the main Element of the tattwa—in this case, Apas, elemental Water, completely bathed in it, and as if all other Elements were non-existent. If this be correctly done, you will find that the thought of any other Element than the one with which you are working will be distinctly distasteful to you.

Having succeeded in obtaining the thought vision of the symbol, continue
. . . with the idea well fixed in your mind of calling before you on the card
a brain picture of some scene or landscape. This, when it first appears, will
probably be vague, but continue to 'make it more real', of whatever nature—
deriving from perhaps imagination or memory—you believe it to be.
Imagination and memory being analogous to the faculty that you are
employing, the probability of their arising at this early stage will be great
. . . the thought picture may eventually become so clear to you (although
this may be a matter of time and much practice) that it will seem as though
the picture were trying to precipitate through the symbol . . . the picture
will be as nearly clear to the perception as a material one might be. But you
can arrive at a great deal by merely receiving the impression of the landscape
as a thought.

. . . follow the rules given . . . until the point where the symbol of the
tattwa has become perfectly vivid to the perception and when you feel as
though you were almost one with the Element. You may modify the earlier
stages of the working by so enlarging the symbol astrally i.e. by the use of
the visual imagination that a human being can pass through it. When very
vivid, and not until then, pass, spring or fly through it . . . till you find yourself
in some place or landscape . . . it would appear well to act exactly as one
would in a physical experience of a landscape, realizing each step as one goes,
not trying to look on both sides at once, or at the back of one's head, but
turning first to the right hand and examining that, then turning to the left,
then right around, and so on . . . the more practically the experiences are
worked, the more chance of success.[2]

In the Golden Dawn and its successsor orders his tattvic vision,
completely derived from tantric texts in all its essentials, was very widely
used as a mode of exploring 'the astral plane', or, if one chooses to use
Jungian terminology, 'investigating the symbolic material present in
the personal and Collective Unconscious'. There is no doubt that in
at least some cases this astral exploration degenerated into a self-indulgent
wallowing in symbolic imagery which, at best, led nowhere, and at
worst led to a psychic inflation in which the reception of supposed
revelations from on high became a substitute for the real life of the spirit.

For some, however, the use of the techniques of tattvic vision was
of great value, resulting in a psychic enrichment. These were those who
never allowed themselves to forget that the astral world is the realm
of illusion, in which the appearance of things is rarely identical with
their inmost nature.

---

2. Flying Roll XXXVI, from which this quotation is taken, appears in the
collection of Golden Dawn instructional manuscripts entitled *Astral
Projection, Magic and Alchemy*, by S. L. MacGregor Mathers and Others (a
new and much enlarged edition of which will shortly be published by
The Aquarian Press).

The methods described above can also be used, in a way which will be subsequently described, to vivify the chakras and, possibly, to develop some of the psychic abilities associated with such a vivification.

In tantric treatises on the chakras many such 'occult powers' are described as being associated with the arousal of a particular chakra or chakras. Many of these treatises contain elements of self-contradiction which either invalidate the statements made, or, perhaps, indicate that such statements must not be understood in a literal sense.

It is generally agreed, however, that the vivification—referred to in one text as kindling the flames—of the chakras is sometimes associated with the acquisition of supernormal abilities as follows:

1. *The Muladhara chakra*: its supposed 'magical power' being complete self-control, mastery of the passions such as lust, envy, anger, hatred, and covetousness. In view of the facts that this chakra is believed to be associated with the perineum, the area of the body between the anus and genitals, and that it is believed to exert subtle influences on the functioning of the gonads and ovaries, it is interesting to note that the passions which are supposed to be brought under control by this chakra's vivification are very largely those which supposedly originate in, or are stimulated by, a misdirected sexual drive.

2. *The Svadisthana chakra*: its magical power being mastery of the astral plane, particularly of that aspect of it which Western ritual magicians symbolize as 'the dark side of the moon'. This latter is, in European occult symbolism, associated with Hecate, in classical mythology the queen of the witches of Thessaly, the evil and adverse aspect of *Diana triformis*,the moon goddess who was believed to manifest herself in three different aspects. As, firstly, the virginal goddess of the hunt, dedicated to eternal chastity; secondly, as 'Diana the many-breasted', goddess of fertility, her ever-flowing breasts sustaining the world—clearly an aspect of Shakti; and finally as Hecate, the crone-goddess who is associated with the converse of fertility—death, barrenness, and abortion.

On one level these three aspects of the moon goddess are no more than personifications of the three stages of the sexual development of the human female; the pre-pubertal child, the fecund mother, and the post-menopausal woman. On a deeper level, however, these three aspects are present, so it is argued, in all women, whatever their age. And on a deeper level still the three aspects of Diana symbolize Shakti as the Unmanifest, Shakti as the Creatrix, Great Mother of All, and Shakti as destroyer—Mother Kali who murders her children and dances on headless and bleeding corpses.

The 'dark side of the moon' aspect of the realm of images which occultists term the astral plane is a reflection, glamorized and often deceptive, of Kali—the destructive side of Shakti. The mastery of the 'dark side of the moon' is therefore one way of apprehending the nature of this aspect of Shakti; those who attempt to attain such a mastery and fail fall victims to the destructive powers of Kali. This is usually a psychic rather than a physical process; the 'dark side of the moon' becomes master instead of servant and a process of ego-inflation follows. Such an inflation is almost an occupational disease in Western occultism. At its worst it can lead to a pathological condition in which the sufferer is unable to cope with the stresses of everyday life; he or she believes himself or herself to have reached a high state of spiritual advancement, or to be the recipient of revelations from the gods, or even to be a 'Secret Chief' or 'Master'. A good example of the lengths to which such self-inflation and delusion can go is provided by a book, first published in 1930, entitled *Light Bearers of Darkness*.

The pseudonymous author of this strange work, compiled from articles published over the years in a periodical entitled *The Patriot*, was an initiate—eventually a chief—of a temple of the Stella Matutina, an offshoot of the Golden Dawn. She became addicted to astral junketings, but failed to engage in any rational analysis of the experiences she underwent. As a result she became a victim of the dark side of the moon, Kali, and suffered delusions that she was being persecuted by 'Black Rosicrucians', agents of a worldwide conspiracy. Her book, with its account of 'revelations' and 'initiations' culminating in psychiatric illness, is well worth reading as an account of Shakti in her incarnation of 'Mother Kali'.

The Svadisthana chakra, then, is particularly associated with Shakti as Destroyer, the dark side of the moon. But surely, it may be objected, the Muladhara chakra is the Shakti-centre, just as the Sahasrara chakra is the Shiva-centre? How, then, can Kali, an aspect of Shakti, be attributed to the Svadisthana chakra?

The answer is quite simple; the Muladhara chakra is peculiarly associated with Shakti—but *all* the chakras contain both Shiva and Shakti elements and, like everything else which exists, or can be conceived to exist, are manifestations of the Shiva/Shakti polarity. Clearly, therefore, the attribution of the 'magical power' of mastery of the astral plane—a reflection of the Kali aspects of Shakti—to the Svadisthana chakra in no way conflicts with the attribution of *all* the aspects of Shakti to the Muladhara chakra.

3. *The Manipura chakra*: the supernormal ability supposedly associated with this chakra is 'the mastery of alchemy and

ceremonial magic'. The association of a mastery of ritual magic with the successful pursuit of alchemy is also found in Western occultism. The ceremonial magic of India and that of the Western world are, at root, identical—the use of light, sound, colour, incense, and other stimuli to so 'enflame the will' of the magician that *change* results. Such change is not necessarily either subjective or exclusively psychological, i.e. a mere change in consciousness. In spite of reductionist attempts to interpret magic as no more than a means of consciousness alteration, a sort of ceremonial psychotherapy, the occult tradition asserts that, rightly used by the skilled student, ritual magic can produce objective changes in the physical environment of the magician, the world of dense matter. It is, however, a matter of fact that most practising magicians of the present day do not produce such changes or, if they do, are careful not to publicize the fact. Such a discretion would be in acccordance with tradition. On the other hand, it may be that the reason so few contemporary students of ritual magic claim to produce objective results is because, in fact, there are no such results. This would not be surprising; if a magician does not believe in the full efficacy of his rites they will, inevitably, be only partly efficacious. Or so, at any rate, occult tradition avers.

Western alchemy can be interpreted in several different ways. As a laboratory technique, concerned with the manipulation of chemical substances, and as a symbolic account of the attainment of psychic wholeness, termed individuation by C. G. Jung and his followers. It can also be understood as a physical process, but one conducted in the interior of the human body, not in a laboratory. This latter is believed to be concerned with polarity in general, and human sexuality in particular. Whether or not such an interpretation of Western alchemy can be considered legitimate is an open question. But there can be no doubt that a good deal of both Indian and Chinese alchemy was of this type, concerned with bodily processes involving human sexual secretions. It is to be presumed that it is alchemy of this sort which can supposedly be mastered as a result of the vivification of the Manipura chakra. Nothing like an adequate description of this tantric alchemy, known as *dhatu vada*, which means 'the substance method', has been attempted by any Western student of Tantra. It suffices to say that this tantric alchemy displays, as might be expected, a concern with polarity which manifests itself in various ways—amongst them a belief that the successful alchemist must combine the consumption of certain carefully prepared medicines with the employment of interior processes and transmutations.

To avoid any misunderstandings it is perhaps best to add that the word 'medicines' is used above in its literal meaning, not in some euphemistic secondary sense. The medicines in question are prepared from plant and mineral substances and have some similarity to the drugs used by Indian physicians who practise traditional Ayurvedic medicine.

4. *The Anahata chakra*; the magical powers and supernormal abilities supposedly associated with this chakra are so many and various that it would be difficult to list them in full. They include the power of manipulating the practitioner's size, i.e. to shrink to the size of an individual molecule or to grow as large as the universe itself, clairvoyance, clairaudience, and invisibility. One tantric text goes so far as to claim that those male adepts who have mastered the powers of the Anahata chakra can 'take over' the bodies of others and 'enjoy their wives'. Most of this sounds either silly or sinister. Perhaps, as argued by some adepts of Tantra, none of this is to be interpreted literally; by, for example, 'becoming infinitely small or infinitely large' may be meant something like 'attaining a mystical understanding of the Shiva/Shakti polarity in things great and small'.

If such powers, in their objectively literal meaning, have been attained by any adepts of Tantra, then such adepts, no doubt for good reason, have never demonstrated them.

5. *The Vishuddha chakra*: the supernormal ability associated with this chakra is 'the attainment of eternal wisdom'—whatever that may mean. It is to be presumed that such wisdom is incommunicable; or, at any rate, that it is rarely communicated. In view of the supposed association between this chakra and the larynx this is somewhat surprising—perhaps it is one more example of the element of paradox which characterizes so much of Tantra.

6. *The Ajna chakra*: the vivification of this chakra supposedly confers 'liberation from the consequences of past actions'. In other words, it removes the adept from his 'karmic liabilities', the spiritual debits which have been incurred in both previous incarnations and his or her present life. This is no more, and no less, than the Christian believes to result from attrition, contrition, and penance.

As far as the tantric is concerned such a removal of karmic burdens implies the attainment of the unitive life, i.e. oneness with the Supreme. Whether one considers this Supreme to be a personal God, as does the Christian, or a Voidness, as does the Buddhist, is a matter of theology. The essential element is well expressed in one Hindu tantric text which affirms that those who control the powers of the Ajna chakra 'dissolve into and are united with the Supreme'.

7. *The Sahasrara chakra:* all supernormal powers pertain to this chakra. Those in whom this chakra is vivified are those in whom 'the marriage of Shiva and Shakti' is continually celebrated and consummated; they are the rulers of space and time, and their mode of being is beyond the full comprehension, so it is said, of all beside themselves.

From the above it will be seen that the supernormal abilities associated with the five tattvas can be summarized as follows:

1. The supernormal power of 'mastery of the passions' is associated with the tattva known as Prithivi. This latter is represented as a yellow square, symbolizes elemental Earth, and is a glyph (symbolic diagram) of the Muladhara chakra.

2. The supernormal power of mastery of the astral world, 'the dark side of the moon', is associated with the tattva known as Apas. The latter is represented as a silver crescent moon, lying on its back, symbolizes elemental water and is a glyph of the Svadisthana chakra.

3. The supernormal power of 'mastery of the techniques of alchemy and ritual magic' is associated with the tattva known as Tejas. The latter is represented as a red-tinged-with-orange equilateral triangle with one angle pointing upwards. It symbolizes elemental Fire.

4. Supernormal powers of many varieties are associated with the tattva known as Vaya. The latter is represented as a sky-blue circle. It symbolizes elemental Air and is a glyph of the Vishuddha chakra.

5. The attainment of 'eternal wisdom' is associated with the tattva known as Akas. The latter is usually represented as a blackish blue 'egg'. It symbolizes 'elemental Spirit'—something like the quintessence of the alchemists—and is a glyph of the Ajna chakra.

Of the supernormal abilities associated with the five tattvas those which are of the greatest interest to most Western occultists are, firstly, the control of the astral plane, and, secondly, the mastery of the techniques of ritual magic and alchemy. As explained above, the first of these is associated with the Svadisthana chakra and the lunar crescent of Apas; the second with the Manipura chakra and the red equilateral triangle of Tejas. In a later chapter a suggestion will be made as to how the two tattvas in question might be used in a way similar to that employed in the Golden Dawn but for a different end; the employment of the methods of Western magic as a specifically tantric technique.

The seven major chakras and the many minor chakras—it will be remembered that according to some sources there are no less than 88,000 of these—are believed to be interconnected by what are called nadis. These are conceived of as conveying subtle energies to and from the chakras in very much the same way as that in which the circulatory system conveys blood to and from the various organs of the physical body.

These subtle energies are regarded as modifications of prana, a 'vital force' which is particularly associated with—although not in any sense a part of—the air we breathe.

Prana is sometimes described as 'the child of sun and moon', which means not the sun and moon of astronomy, but the principles of which they are expressions, Shiva and Shakti. A considerable number of tantric techniques are intended to concentrate prana, or one of the more 'vital airs' of which it is believed to be constituted, in the body of the individual practitioner. 'Body' in this context means the 'subtle body', of which the chakras are the vital organs and the nadis the veins, arteries, and nerves.

These techniques, largely concerned with breath control, are described in a later chapter. Here it is sufficient to say that it is these techniques which are of real importance in the context of Tantra, not the theories concerning prana and its constituents which are associated with those techniques. The concept of prana is merely one of a number of possible explanations of the fact that such techniques have been found to be efficacious.

The same is true of the entire system of esoteric physiology which has been outlined above. While, as will be shown in the next chapter, there are worldwide traditions concerning the existence of a network of 'psychic centres' associated with the human body, there is no absolute necessity for the tantric practitioner to believe in the objective existence of such centres, let alone in the 88,000 chakras of some tantric theorists. The chakras may be no more than mental constructs—but the fact remains that the tantric adept finds it useful to *behave as if they existed*. And, what is more, there is considerable evidence, much of it admittedly anecdotal, that they do exist.

CHAPTER FIVE

Chakras, Secret Traditions, and the Golden Dawn

The system of occult anatomy and physiology which has been outlined in the preceding chapter has sometimes been understood—or, rather, misunderstood—in a crudely physical sense. Thus, for example, one eminent nineteenth-century historian and educationalist confidently affirmed that Hindu religious teachers held beliefs about the functions of the human body 'which would disgrace the most ignorant rural blacksmith'. This statement undoubtedly resulted from a naïve and unduly literal reading of Hindu mystical texts. It typified the arrogant self-satisfaction which characterized Victorian attitudes towards oriental religious teachings.

Nevertheless, it has to be admitted that some tantric gurus have propagated literalistic, vulgarized, and inaccurate versions of the esoteric physiology of the authentic tantric tradition. Pupils of such gurus have been taught, for example, that the chakras are physical organs in exactly the same way as the kidneys are physical organs, and that the subtle energy pathways of the nadis are, quite literally, hollow passages through which air is conveyed to the base of the spine.

Dayanand Saraswati, founder of the Hindu reformist group known as the Arya Samaj, began his life of spiritual activity as the pupil of a guru of this type. Filled with the desire to observe with his physical sight the chakras and the pathways between them he dissected a human body. What he found bore no resemblance to what he expected to find; he decided that all he has been taught concerning yogic and tantric occult physiology was 'superstitious rubbish' and came to the conclusion that all Hindu literature save the Vedas was utterly worthless. In other words, both Dayanand Saraswati and his guru had made the same literalist errors as the European scholars who despised their culture.

It is unlikely that many Western occultists of the present day would fall into the same trap. But it is easy for them to go to the other, arguable, but perhaps equally erroneous, extreme and adopt a reductionist viewpoint from which the entire chakra system is seen as no more than a symbolic model of psychic realities—i.e. a diagrammatic representation of modes of consciousness, and psychic processes, which have no material existence but are present in the minds of human beings as 'feelings', 'intuitions', and 'ideas'.

Such a viewpoint, which reduces the ancient wisdom of Tantra to little more than a series of psychological quirks and oddities, has not been entirely confined to those (such as Jungian analytical psychologists) who have approached the esoteric tradition from *outside* that tradition. On the contrary, the influence of the subjectivist approach can be discerned in the writings of many dedicated occultists. Amongst these was the late Dion Fortune who, as will be shown later, may have been seriously misled by it when she attempted to correlate Hindu esoteric physiology with what she called 'the Western Esoteric Tradition'—i.e. the synthesis of European magical theory and technique constructed by S. L. MacGregor Mathers and other leading personalities of the Hermetic Order of the Golden Dawn and its derivatives.

Such an exclusively psychological interpretation of the physiological teachings of tantrism is in clear contradiction to not only the tantric tradition itself, but to the traditions of many other systems of psycho-spiritual development, Eastern and Western. Such systems are remarkably consistent with one another and insist upon the objective existence of centres of psychic energy closely associated with specific areas of the physical body.

Thus, for example, certain ancient Greek writings contain guarded references to 'hidden centres' within the human body, these seeming to indicate the existence of a secret tradition—possibly derived from ancient Egypt—concerning 'physical power centres' through the manipulation of which ordinary human beings can enter into communion with the gods and share their mode of existence.

The secret tradition of a mystical process or processes involving the *whole* man—the physical body as well as the intellect, conscious will, emotions, immortal soul, etc.—survived the decline of paganism and deeply influenced the mysticism of both Islam and orthodox Christianity. In the latter case the influence is most apparent in the Heyschasts[1] and their 'Prayer of the Heart'. 'Heart' in this context means

---

1. The Heyschasts were, and are, mystics of the Eastern Church who, in accordance with mystical traditions which have been in existence since the time of the pseudo-Dionysius, accept that God is, in essence, directly unknowable. Nevertheless, they believe that it is possible to know God through his 'energies', and have developed many techniques, described in detail in a vast compilation entitled the *Philokalia*, for arriving at such a knowledge.

not the emotions, but the entire human being—spirit, intellect, feelings, and, above all, material body—and an integral part of Heyschasm was, and still is, the use of particular modes of breathing and the adoption of a specific bodily posture. These are dealt with in some detail in Chapter Eight, which gives practical advice on tantric meditation and yoga. It suffices here to say that the ritualized breathing of Heyschasm is essentially identical with pranayama and that the posture adopted is one which involves the vivification of the chakras, particular emphasis being placed upon concentration on the epigastric plexus, which is, as described on page 56, associated with the Manipura chakra.

It is not only their tendency to 'psychologize the somatic'—that is, to interpret physical aspects of spiritual disciplines in purely mental terms—that has led some Western occultists astray in their efforts to reconcile tantric esoteric physiology with modern qabalism. They have also been misled by (a) a slavish adherence to the ancient, but extremely rough and ready, method of attributing the various parts of the human body to the qabalistic Tree of Life by drawing a man's body against the outline of the Tree, and (b) a tendency to over-simplify the way in which human physical functions should be attributed to the component elements. Thus, for example, most contemporary qabalists attribute the genitals and physical sexuality to the ninth sephirah (Yesod, 'The Foundation') of the Tree of Life on the basis of both 'the body against the Tree' and a supposed traditional attribution. In reality, however, the traditional attributions concerning sexuality are much more complex than this and some of them refer to sephiroth other than Yesod.

There are three well known methods of correlating the seven major chakras with the sephiroth of the qabalah. The first is contained in Column CXVIII of 777, the compilation of qabalistic correspondences compiled by Aleister Crowley and first published in 1909. Most of the lists contained in 777 are no more than tabulations of material found scattered through various of the 'Knowledge Lectures' and other instructional manuscripts of the Hermetic Order of the Golden Dawn. This is not the case with Column CXVIII, however, and it is to be presumed that this column was compiled by Crowley on the basis of the intuitions and researches of himself and Alan Bennett, his occult teacher. The second system of the chakra/sephiroth correlation is contained in various writings of the late Major-General J. F. C. Fuller, notably his books on yoga and the qabalah. Fuller had at one time been a pupil of Crowley and his system is clearly a variant of that contained in 777. The final, and most recent, is that which Dion Fortune expounded on pp. 81-83 of her book *The Mystical Qabalah*, first published in 1935.

The variations between these three methods can be seen clearly in the following table:

Chakra	Qabalistic Correlation According to		
	Crowley	Fuller	Fortune
Muladhara	Yesod	Malkuth	Malkuth
Svadisthana	Hod	Yesod	Yesod
Manipura	Netzach	Geburah	Tiphereth
Anahata	Chesed, Geburah and Tiphareth	Chesed	Tiphereth
Vishuddha	Binah	Binah	Daath
Ajna	Chokmah	Chokmah	Daath
Sahasrara	Kether	Kether	Kether

Those readers who are acquainted with Crowley's correlation only through the account given by Dion Fortune will be surprised to note that in the above table it is indicated that Crowley equated the Manipura chakra with Netzach and the Anahata chakras with the three sephiroth, Chesed, Geburah, and Tiphereth. This is in complete contradiction to a statement made by Dion Fortune who wrote that 'Tiphereth . . . represents the solar plexus and breast; it therefore seems reasonable to attribute to it the Manipura and Anahata Chakras, as Crowley does' (*Mystical Qabalah*, p. 82).

In spite of this categorical statement the attributions of the chakras to the sephiroth in 777 are as shown in the above table and *not* as described in *The Mystical Qabalah*; I can only presume that Dion Fortune had misunderstood the significance of a bracket which, in fact, pertains to Column CXVI, the 'Egyptian Attributions of Parts of the Soul.'

It will be noticed that while Crowley attributed the Muladhara chakra to Yesod, Dion Fortune and J. F. C. Fuller were in agreement that it should be attributed to Malkuth, the sephirah which represents the world of dense matter. Fuller supported this attribution by stating that the Muladhara chakra is often symbolically pictured as a four-petalled lotus; these petals, he said, represented the alchemical elements of Earth, Air, Fire, and Water. He could have strengthened his argument by pointing out that the tattva known as Prithivi symbolizes elemental Earth and is traditionally associated with the Muladhara chakra.

Dion Fortune supported this argument, but added to it a curiously psychoanalytical note which seemed to suggest that Crowley had 'an infantile mind' in which 'the functions of reproduction and excretion are confused.'

The real basis of the Fuller/Fortune attribution seems to have been, firstly, a traditional qabalistic description of Malkuth as corresponding to 'the buttocks and anus of the perfected man', and, secondly, a belief that the perineum—the area of the body supposedly associated with the Muladhara chakra—can be equated with the anus. There seems to be no real justification for this belief; the tantric tradition quite specifically asserts that the parts of the body which have an especial relationship with the Muladhara chakra are the testes and the ovaries, not the anus and the buttocks. If anybody was confusing excretion and reproduction it was Fuller and Fortune, not Crowley.

The Muladhara chakra has, as was explained earlier in relation to the tattvas, a relationship with 'elemental Earth', which undoubtedly corresponds with the Malkuth of the qabalists. But the essential thing about the Muladhara chakra is that it is the dwelling place of Kundalini, the coiled serpent-power of Shakti, the dynamic element in polarity relationships in general and human sexuality in particular.

There is a general agreement amongst qabalists that physical sexuality pertains to Yesod, and, if this is so, there can be no doubt that Crowley was perfectly correct in attributing the Muladhara chakra to that sephirah.

There is, in fact, no good reason to feel, as Fuller and Fortune seem to have done, that Malkuth *must* be equated with some chakra. Malkuth symbolizes the material universe, and none of the chakras belong to that universe, although, of course, they supposedly influence it. It is perfectly reasonable, however, to regard the Muladhara/Yesod chakra as *subsuming* Malkuth, just as the 'formative forces' of Yesod in a sense subsume the world of dense matter.

Fuller and Fortune's attribution of the Muladhara chakra to Malkuth virtually forced them to attribute the Svadisthana chakra to Yesod, the ninth sephirah. On the face of it this attribution has many attractions. Yesod is the sphere of reproduction, physical sexuality, and certain aspects of psychism which relate to lunar symbolism, and the tattva associated with this chakra is in the shape of a crescent moon lying on its back. Additionally, the supernormal ability particularly associated with the vivification of the Svadisthana chakra is the mastery of those aspects of the astral world which are sometimes symbolized as 'the dark side of the moon'.

However, in spite of its crescent moon shape, the tattva known as Apas and associated with the Svadishthana chakra does not symbolize lunar forces but 'elemental Water'. The concepts associated with elemental Water have certain lunar aspects, but they are not specifically lunar, and the astral worlds pertain not only to the sephirah Yesod, but also to the sephiroth Hod and Netzach. Dion Fortune was well aware of this and referred to the trinity of Netzach-Hod-Yesod as 'the Astral World'. There is therefore nothing intrinsically improbable in Crowley's attribution of the Svadisthana chakra to Hod.

Such an attribution is supported by an old mode of classifying the nine sephiroth from Kether to Malkuth in terms of the three 'mother letters' of the Hebrew alphabet. These are Aleph, attributed to Air, Shin attributed to Fire, and Mem, attributed to Water. The three sephiroth classified under Shin, Fire, are Chokmah, Geburah and Netzach. The first of these, Chokmah, is regarded as the 'Root of Fire', its burning strength reflected as the martial fire of Geburah and the amatory fire of Netzach. The three sephiroth classified under Aleph, Air, are Kether, Tiphereth, and Yesod, while those attributed to Mem, Water, are Binah, the Root of Water, Chesed, and Hod. It is therefore clear that the tattva associated with the Svadisthana chakra is more in conformity with an equation with Hod than with Yesod.

However, as the 'astral triangle' of Netzach-Hod-Yesod has its focus in Yesod there could be no objection to the Fortune/Fuller attribution provided that this was regarded as a special aspect of Yesod and it was agreed that the Muladhara chakra should also be equated with Yesod, not Malkuth.

Crowley probably attributed the Manipura chakra to Netzach because of the fiery elemental qualities of the latter. It seems more satisfactory, however, to follow Dion Fortune in attributing both the Manipura and Anahata chakras to Tiphereth. This is not really in conflict with Fuller's attribution of these two chakras to Chesed and Geburah. For Tiphereth is the focus, the concentration point, of the triangle Chesed-Geburah-Tiphereth, just as Yesod is the focus of the astral triangle.

Both J. F. C. Fuller and Crowley attributed the Vishuddha and Ajna chakras to Binah and Chokmah respectively. Dion Fortune attributed both to Daath, Knowledge, a mysterious 'invisible sephirah' which has been the subject of much speculation amongst contemporary occultists. As Daath is regarded as a conjoining of the influences of Chokmah and Binah there is no real disagreement on these attributions.

The same applies to the Sahasrara chakra, which all agree should be equated with Kether.

From the above it will now be clear that it is possible to outline a system of chakra/sephirah equation which is confined to the Middle Pillar of the Tree of Life. This is as follows:

Chakra	Equivalent Middle Pillar Sephirah
Muladhara	Yesod (subsuming Malkuth)
Svadisthana	Yesod (as focus of astral triangle)
Manipura	Tiphereth

Chakra	Equivalent Middle Pillar Sephirah
Anahata	Tiphereth
Vishuddha	Daath (as focus of Chokmah and Binah)
Ajna	Daath (as focus of Chokmah and Binah)
Sahasrara	Kether

(Note: Daath is not shown on diagrams of the Tree of Life)

This equation with the Middle Pillar of the Tree of Life is not altogether satisfactory as an intellectual construct but, as will be demonstrated in a later chapter, it enables a well-known Western occult process known as the 'Exercise of the Middle Pillar' to be adapted to tantric workings.

In considering the equation between the chakras of Tantra and the sephiroth of qabalism I have given considerable weight to the opinions of Crowley. How far, in fact, can Crowley be considered a tantric is a matter of debate. Some would say that he was a supreme tantric adept, others would affirm that his teachings were a gross perversion of Tantra and that he used tantric concepts to excuse his own immorality.

Crowley, as everyone knows, was a dedicated and exceptionally intelligent occultist. It is also a matter of common knowledge that he was sexually active from a very early age, that he was at times promiscuous, and that he regarded chastity as the worst and most inexplicable of perversions. But, of course, much sexual activity by an occultist does not necessarily indicate an inclination towards Tantra, any more than rigid dieting by an occultist necessarily implies asceticism. In the former case he or she may simply be, like a great many other people, addicted to promiscuity; in the latter case he or she may be suffering from anorexia nervosa. On the other hand the fact that a particular occultist enjoys sex for its own sake does not mean that he or she cannot, on occasion, be using sex as a sacrament as well as to obtain the physical pleasures of orgasm.

Crowley was a man who enjoyed his physical appetites—food, particularly curry, drink, particularly burgundy and port, tobacco, particularly Latakia matured in rum; and sex of any variety.

As a young man, an initiate of the Golden Dawn, Crowley was influenced by the asceticism of MacGregor Mathers and seems to have struggled, often ineffectually, against his own sexual appetites; in an early occult diary, for example, he recorded that his sleep had been disturbed as a result of 'obsession by Venus' and that he had used 'banishing rituals' as a countermeasure.

Within two or three years he decided that the expression of an individual's sexual tastes, whatever their nature, was no barrier to spiritual advancement. At this stage, however, he seems to have had no conception of anything like the physical techniques of Tantra; while he had received instruction in meditation and yoga from qualified Buddhist and Hindu teachers, those teachers were all ascetics, their mental attitudes the very converse of those associated with Tantra. At no time of his life, in fact, was Crowley the pupil of either Buddhist, Hindu, or Jain, tantrics.

Crowley first seems to have decided that sexuality could be incorporated into occult rituals as a result of reading some of the messier grimoires—text books of ritual magic, some white, some black, most of an unpleasant shade of grey—for his first attempt to use sex for occult purposes was in the course of a ceremony which most people would regard as being of the nature of black magic.

At the time Crowley was engaged in a long and acrimonious quarrel with MacGregor Mathers and W. B. Yeats, the details of which are outside the scope of this book. Crowley had decided that Mathers was subjecting him to an 'astral attack'. Whether or not the alleged attack ever took place is uncertain; but there is no doubt that Mathers disliked Crowley quite enough to launch such an attack and that Crowley's pet dogs had died in unusual and mysterious circumstances—perhaps, as Crowley claimed, as the result of malign occult influences, more probably of poison. Crowley, having decided that black magic was being used against him, determined to employ similar methods against Mathers and devised a ritual for that purpose.

This ceremony involved the evocation of Beelzebub, one of the legendary Princes of Hell. The text of the rite, which survives in only fragmentary form, indicates that Rose, Crowley's wife, should be kneeling naked, 'arse as high as possible', throughout the duration of the ceremony. It is possible that Crowley intended the curiously positioned Rose to be no more than an unusual ornament for his temple, a human bait for Beelzebub. But it is more likely that some sexual act, presumably of a nature which Beelzebub might find to his hellish taste, was incorporated into the evocation.

While Crowley undoubtedly possessed some clairvoyant powers— i.e. the ability to 'see visions' or 'have pictorial hallucinations'—he preferred to use 'seers' who reported their vision to him. As a preparation for their visionary experiences the seers, usually, but not invariably, women, were excited by drink, sexual activity, and, on many occasions, psychedelic drugs, typically cannabis or anhalonium (mescal buttons).

While alcohol and sexual intercourse are an integral part of *some* tantric rites, and cannabis is usually taken as a preliminary to such rites, there is nothing specifically tantric in using the stimuli of drink, drugs and sex as a means of overloading the central nervous system and inducing a dissociation of consciousness in which visions are seen.

One cannot, therefore, claim Crowley as an authentic practitioner of Tantra on this account.

Nevertheless, there are certain aspects of Crowley's teachings which must, I think, be considered tantric or, at the very least, in total conformity with Tantra. These aspects of Crowley's system are to be found in codified, but not always easily understandable, form in those instructional texts compiled by Crowley and his associates which can be described as the tantric *Libres*.

Over the period of almost half a century during which Crowley taught his Magic—a synthetic mystical/magical system which could well be described as Neognosticism—he wrote many inspirational and/or didactic works which he called *Libres*. Some of these are full length books, others little more than half a page or so text. Of these the ones which can legitimately be considered to be at least quasi-tantric are five in number. They are:

> *Of the Art of Magic*
> *Of the Nature of the Gods*
> *Of the Homunculus*
> *The Book of the Unveiling of the Sangraal*
> *Of the Secret Marriages of Gods and Men*

The 'Tantra' techniques which Crowley expounded in these works he derived from a German source which claimed, almost certainly falsely, to have a shadowy ancestry leading back to the Knights Templar of the Middle Ages. The founder, or supposed founder, of this German organization was alleged to have received instruction in sexual magic from a Hindu teacher or teachers. There is no good reason to be unduly sceptical of this latter claim.

On to the methods he had learned from his German teachers, Crowley grafted a philosophical structure which seems almost identical to that associated with the Tantra of northern India. This Crowleyan philosophy regards the universe and its component parts in exactly the same way as they are regarded in the Tantra of Bengal—as side effects of the eternal game played by Shakti and Shiva. The terminology, however, is different.

Crowley called Shakti by the name of Nuit, the Egyptian star-goddess to whom previous reference has been made. Shiva he called by another Egyptian name, 'Hadit'. The 'concrete incarnation' of Shakti was called 'Babalon' by Crowley, that of Shiva he called 'the Beast', a name which he specifically applied to himself, which seems both odd and arrogant.

It is unlikely, however, that he, Aleister Crowley, the man whose feet walked the streets of London and New York, was foolish enough to think that he was Shiva, the male principle of the cosmic duality—

although it has to be admitted that in moods of exaltation he sometimes wrote and spoke as if this was the case. It seems rather more probable that he believed that there existed an element in his psycho-spiritual makeup—an element that had been developed as the result of a series of progressive illuminations—which was an avatar, a manifestation of Shiva.

Many of these supposed illuminations are to be found recorded in *The Vision and the Voice*, a work which Crowley first printed in his magazine *The Equinox* before 1914, and which had been compiled by himself and a disciple, largely on the basis of certain experiences they had undergone together in the deserts of North Africa. It is in this work that Crowley's quasi-tantric philosophy is most clearly expressed, not in the tantric *Libres* referred to above.

These latter are very largely concerned with techniques. These bear certain marked similarities to those used by left-handed tantrics, but are by no means identical with them. In some ways they are undoubtedly cruder than their Indian analogues; there is less emphasis, for example, on the preliminaries to explicitly sexual rites. In part this was almost certainly because Crowley wished to strip Tantra down to its essential core—the use of the senses to transcend sensuality and achieve adeptship—in order to give it a universal validity free of associations with particular sets of cultural conventions such as those typical of Hindu society.

But as far as Tantra was concerned Crowley was no mere simplifier. He subtracted some things from the tradition as he knew it, but added others, making innovations which, while they may be compatible with Bengali tradition, seem to have no oriental analogues.

Notable amongst these innovations was an autoerotic technique which he expounded generally in the *Liber* entitled *Of the Secret Marriages of Gods and Men* and, more particularly, in the chapter of that work called 'Of Great Marriages'. When examining the text of this and Crowley's other tantric *Libres* it must be held in mind that, like many other tantric treatises, they employ a 'twilight language' in which words are given a secondary, tantric significance.

It is very easy, however, to break Crowley's code. Thus in the 'Great Marriages' chapter of *Of the Secret Marriages*, referred to above in relation to autoeroticism, the word 'purge' is not used in its primary, excretory sense but in reference to orgasm. Similarly, in the eleventh chapter of the same work the phrase 'Evocation by the Wand' means an act of masturbation in which the operator's imaginary partner is an immaterial entity such as an angel. The 'Marrow of the Wand', referred to in the same chapter, simply means sexual fluids.

The code words and phrases employed to express the sexual concepts in both the tantric *Libres* and Crowley's more general writings were often derived from the terminology of Western alchemy. Thus Crowley used the archaic word for an alchemical furnace (athanor) as a code word for the penis, while the word 'cucurbite', a piece of laboratory equipment used by alchemists for purposes of distillation, he used as a code word for the vulva. The male sexual discharge was referred to in the tantric *Libres* as 'the serpent' or 'the blood of the red lion', phrases which in texts concerned with physical alchemy, of the type conducted in a laboratory, refer to metallic salts. Similarly the fluids which lubricate the vagina were referred to as the 'menstruum of the gluten', while the mixture of this with semen Crowley called 'the First Matter' and, after it had supposedly been imbued with magical powers by the processes outlined in the tantric *Libres*, 'the Elixir'.

These alchemical words and phrases were not arbitrarily chosen. Crowley believed, rightly or wrongly, that many Western alchemical texts were concerned, not with chemical processes intended to produce a mysterious stone which could transmute base metals into gold, but with sexual techniques, essentially identical with those of left-handed Tantra, the use of which would result in psychic transmutation.

Such a variant of European alchemy, a sort of Western Tantra, *may* have existed. As was said earlier, polarity symbolism is apparent in many alchemical texts, and it seems probable that at least some alchemists were concerned with interior transformations rather than the physical transmutations desired by alchemical laboratory workers. It is possible that a few of these 'psychic alchemists', a minority of a minority, practised something very like Tantra, interpreting alchemical polarity symbolism in a semi-literal way.

There are so many resemblances between the techniques taught in the tantric *Libres* and those employed in oriental Tantra that it is difficult to avoid the conclusion that Crowley was an authentic, if unorthodox, tantric.

It would be possible, of course, to argue that as a tantric Crowley was not just unorthodox, but perverted—there are spiritual paths which lead to the depths as there are those which lead to the heights—but a tantric I am sure he was.[2]

Crowley, as was said earlier, had never received tantric instructions from an Eastern teacher and his knowledge of left-handed techniques had been derived from German sources. Curiously enough he may

---

2. Those who wish to examine the tantric *Libres* for themselves will find the text of *Of the Art of Magic* printed as an appendix to *Crowley on Christ* (London, 1974). Versions of the other tantric *Libres* are printed in *The Secret Rituals of the OTO* (London and New York, 1973).

well have learned something of Tantra while he was a member of the Golden Dawn. For while the sexual techniques of left-handed Tantra would have been regarded as black magic by most of the leadership of that society—MacGregor Mathers attached so much importance to chastity that he never consummated his marriage—a certain amount of tantric theory and (non-sexual) practice was incorporated into the Order's teachings.

The tantric elements in the Golden Dawn system were derived from an early publication of the Theosophical Society entitled *Nature's Finer Forces*, a Bengali tantric text translated into English by a certain Rama Prasad. It seems likely that those most prominent in the Theosophical Society at the time of the book's first publication were not fully aware of its tantric provenance; for Madame Blavatsky and her associates thoroughly disapproved of what little they knew of Tantra and described its devotees as 'hypocrites'. This attitude has persisted until the present day amongst the followers of Madame Blavatsky, at least as far as tantric techniques involving physical sexuality are concerned. Thus, for example, W. Y. Evans-Wentz, an authority on Buddhist Tantra whose edition of the *Tibetan Book of the Dead* became the object of something of a hippy cult in the 1960s, went so far as to refer to the practitioners of such techniques as 'those hypocrites who follow the left-hand path in Bengal and elsewhere'. Such a total rejection of left-handed Tantra as 'hypocritical' seems to have been largely confined to Theosophists, and it is interesting to note that the late Sir John Woodroffe, a practising Catholic who wrote on Tantra under both his own name and that of 'Arthur Avalon', endeavoured to understand left-handed Tantra in its own terms.

What those Victorian members of the Theosophical Society who bought copies of *Nature's Finer Forces* made of the tantric treatise which is its core is uncertain—probably they looked upon it with the same mingled awe and incomprehension with which they seem to have regarded anything with an Indian provenance, from the *Vedas* to Benares brasswork of the sort of which Madame Blavatsky's disciple Colonel Olcott was so fond. But one Theosophist, who was later to win renown as a ritual magician, was not only impressed by the book but studied it. The magician in question was S. L. MacGregor Mathers, and, surprisingly, what seems to have particularly impressed him about the book was that it provided him with a new interpretation of a novel entitled *Zanoni*.

Zanoni, first published in 1842, had been written by Edward Bulwer Lytton (1803-73), who combined authorship with politics—he was for a time Colonial Secretary—and was sufficiently interested in the occult to be on friendly terms with the French magician Eliphas Lévi and to accept the position of Grand Patron of the *Societas Rosicruciana in Anglia*, the 'Rosicrucian Society in England'.

Like *A Strange Story*, which Lytton published in the 1860s, *Zanoni* could be described as an attempt to give a 'quasi-scientific colouring to old fashioned magic'. The character of Zanoni, the novel's protagonist, was loosely based on some of the legends surrounding the eighteenth-century adventurer—thought by some to be an occult 'Master'—who called himself the Comte de St Germain. The plot of *Zanoni* is of extreme and tedious complexity; it suffices to say that Zanoni employs supernormal powers to defeat the machinations of a number of villains, amongst them the Prince di D____, a descendant of the Visconti family who, rather oddly, knows the secrets of the poisons employed by the Borgias.

On one occasion the Prince endeavours to murder Zanoni by administering to him the Borgia poison dissolved in a goblet of Cyprus wine—'The cypress', mutters one of the Prince's aides, 'is a proper emblem of the grave.' Zanoni imbibes the poison but is unaffected by it; one of the many incidents in the novel in which he exhibits his supernatural powers.

Mathers was deeply impressed by *Zanoni* and seems to have mentally identified himself with its hero—according to report his wife went so far as to nickname him 'Zan.' For reasons which are not clear to me Mathers believed, or at least, half-believed, that the supposed novel was not a novel at all but a fictionalized account of the actual activities of some adept. The question then arose in Mathers' mind as to how Zanoni achieved his powers; for example, the ability to overcome poison.

Mathers found the answer to his question in *Nature's Finer Forces*. Zanoni, he decided, had mastered the power of manipulating the subtle energy flows described in that book and associated with the tattvas and chakras. He wrote:

Zanoni . . . overcame the effects of the poisoned wine of the Prince di D____ as follows . . . he brought the Water, Apas, tattva into course, directed it with the full force of his trained will towards the poisoned wine, and consequently the burning heat of the poison was counteracted for a very long time, and before it could recover strength enough to act on the system, it was there no longer.

This seems a little obscure. What I think Mathers meant was as follows. The Borgian poison was of a fiery, burning nature. Zanoni concentrated on the tattva, Apas, which symbolizes elemental Water. This tattva, it will be remembered, is symbolized by a crescent moon lying on its back and is particularly associated with the Svadisthana chakra. From this chakra Zanoni directed a stream of Apas-energy at the fiery poison dissolved in the wine. The 'watery' quality of this energy temporarily dowsed the 'fire' of the poison, and by the time the Apas-energy had exhausted itself, and the fire of the poison had rekindled, the poison, was, in Mathers' coy phrase, 'there no longer'—i.e. Zanoni had excreted it.

Mathers explained other incidents in Zanoni on the same lines, all of equal value—or worthlessness. He himself was so impressed with such explanations that he compiled a summary of the teachings contained in the tantric text included in *Nature's Finer Forces*, entitled it *On the Tattwas of the Eastern School*, made it an official Golden Dawn instructional document, and incorporated much of its teachings into that Order's system.[3]

Thus, for example, the techniques of astral vision, described in the preceding chapter and widely used in the Golden Dawn and its successor fraternities, such as the Stella Matutina, involved the use of the five tattvas as described in Mathers' *On the Tattwas of the Eastern School*. Similarly, elaborate 'tattvic tide-tables' supposedly of solar and lunar tattvic energies were compiled. These were and are believed to be of great importance to the practical occultist and have sometimes been described as one of the most closely guarded secrets of the Western Esoteric Tradition. Thus, for example, in paragraph 17 of Chapter XXIV of her book *The Mystical Qabalah* the late Dion Fortune claimed that they have 'always been kept secret', that they 'concern the secret workings', and are only 'given after initiation.' In reality, however, the source from which such charts have been compiled, the tantric text incorporated into *Nature's Finer Forces*, has been available in printed form for a century or so.

Mathers' *On the Tattwas of the Eastern School* is, then, a basically tantric text which has deeply influenced modern Western occultism. As such it is of deep and abiding interest to those Westerners who wish to approach, study, and, perhaps, practise, Tantra in terms of their own tradition.

The essence of *On the Tattwas* can be summarized as follows (indented passages are direct quotations from the Mathers document, any passages in square brackets are my own comments or explanations upon either these quotations or the summary I give; the latter is neither indented nor in brackets):

---

3. It is quite certain that Mathers was extremely impressed by *Nature's Finer Forces* and that he incorporated its teachings into the Golden Dawn system. It may be, however, that it was not he but Brodie Innes who compiled *On the Tattwas*. In this connection see Appendix A, 'Brodie Innes and the Tattvas.

There are five tattwas or principles (a) Akasa-Ether, (2) Vayu, the Aerial principle, (3) Tejas the principle of light and heat, (4) Apas, the Water principle, and (5) Prithivi, the Earth principle.

But the First Cause is the Great Controller of all things, the One Light, the Formless . . .

[The tattwas are, of course, as listed in my preceding chapter save that Akasa is attributed to Ether—a now outmoded concept as far as physics is concerned, rather than 'elemental Spirit'. The 'First Cause' can be identified with the Shiva/Shakti duality.]

The 'First Cause' manifests itself in the body (which in this context means both the physical body and other, more subtle, vehicles of consciousness) as ten forces which permeate all the nerves (i.e. the nadis, the invisible energy channels which supposedly interconnect the chakras). The ten forces are listed as:

(1) Prana   —in the breast
(2) Apana   —about the excretory organs
(3) Samana   —in the navel
(4) Undana   —middle of the throat
(5) Vyana   —pervading the whole body
(6) Kurmana   —the eyes, helping them open
(7) Kirkala   —in the stomach, producing hunger
(8) Nag   —whence comes vomiting
(9) Devadatta   —causes yawning
(10) Dhananjaya   —that which does not leave the body after death.

[As with all tantric texts the above listing of the functions of the forces and the parts of the body associated with them must not be taken too literally. Thus Kurmana is described as helping the eyes to keep open, which is probably an indication that it is supposedly the formative force which underlies the quality of alertness; Kirkala, described as 'producing hunger' may represent the formative force behind the survival instinct; and Nag, 'whence comes vomiting', may indicate the forces which manifest themselves in reflex actions.]

The ten forces have their play in all the 'nerves' (nadis) and of these the three most important are:

(1) Ida   —the left bronchus (lung)
(2) Pingala   —the right bronchus (lung)
(3) Sushumna   —in the middle

[The above is a considerable oversimplification of tantric physiology. The nadi known as Sushumna is conceived of as having its origin in the Muladhara chakra and running up the 'subtle body' in the same way as the centre of the spine runs up the physical body. The Ida nadi is conceived of as originating in a subtle analogue of the *right* testicle/ovary, curling round the Sushumna like a coiled serpent, and terminating in the left nostril. Pingala is regarded as also being coiled around the Sushumna, rising from the *left* testicle/ovary and terminating in the right nostril.]

> The key to all . . . lies in . . . drawing the air through the Ida, the Pingala, and the Sushumna. When the Air is drawn through the Ida it is felt coming in or going out through the left nostril. When through the Sushumna it is felt through both nostrils simultaneously . . . when the breath is in the Ida it gives coolness to the body . . . when in the Pingala it gives heat to the body . . .

[The literal meaning of the above is, quite clearly, an excessively physical exposition of the esoteric physiology associated with Tantra. What was in the mind of the original author of the text cannot be known, but most contemporary tantrics, East or West, would regard the 'Air' referred to as being a vital energy which, while absorbed into the subtle body at the same time as the oxygen of the atmosphere is absorbed into the red corpuscles of the bloodstream, is in no way part of the physical air we breathe.]

> The Lunar month, it is well known, is divided into two parts, the fortnight of the Waxing and the fortnight of the Waning. On the first fortnight . . . just as sunrise on the first day the Breath must come into the left nostril and must be so for three days successively. At the beginning of the fourth day the Breath must come through the right nostril and must do so for the three succeeding days, when again the seventh day must begin with the Moon breath [another name for the 'breath' associated with the left nostril and the Ida nadi], and so on in the same order . . .
>
> But how long is our breath to remain in one nostril? For five Gharis, or two hours. Thus when the first day of the Bright fortnight begins with the Moon breath, after five Gharis the Sun breath [i.e. the 'breath' associated with the Pingala nadi] must set in, and this must again change into the Moon breath after the same interval of time. So on for every day.
>
> Again, the first day of the dark fortnight must begin with the Sun breath, and proceed in the same way, changing after five Gharis . . .

[All this sounds confused and is certainly, on first reading, confusing. Whatever the literal meaning of the text we can be quite sure that no normal human being breathes through only one nostril at a time, changing nostrils every two hours. What Mathers and his successors, such as Dion Fortune, understood it to mean when they compiled their 'tattvic tide-tables' was that tides of subtle 'solar' and 'lunar' energies alternate every two hours as follows:

(1) The first three days of the waxing moon—i.e. the period of

approximately a fortnight from the appearance of a new moon until the full moon—commences with a two-hour period, beginning at sunrise on the first day, during which the lunar energies associated with the Ida nadi are at full strength. This is succeeded by a two-hour dominance of the solar energies, then two hours of the lunar, and so on, for a period of approximately 72 hours ending at sunrise on the fourth day. The final period of roughly two hours is, of course, one in which solar forces are dominant.

(2) This is immediately succeeded, beginning at sunrise of the fourth day, by another two hours of solar influence. This alternates with lunar domination, the 'tide' changing every two hours, until the end of another 72 hours, ending with a period of lunar influence.

(3) The cycle in (1) is then repeated, then the cycle in (2), until the period of waxing culminates with the full moon.

(4) During the period of the waning moon the above process continues but with a polarity reversal—i.e. the first day begins with solar dominance, the fourth with lunar dominance, and so on.

Whether such solar and lunar energy flows enjoy an objective existence is a matter of debate; there is no doubt, however, that some occultists have found it useful to assume that they do.]

For five Gharis . . . or two hour periods, the Tattwas have their course. In the first we have Akasa, in the second Vayu, in the third Tejas, in the fourth Apas, in the fifth Prithivi. Thus in one night and day, or sixty Gharis, we have twelve courses of these five Tattwas each remaining one Ghari (i.e. 24 minutes) and returning again in two hours. There are again a further five subdivisions of each Tattwa in a Ghari. Thus, Akasa is subdivided into Akas-Akasa; Akas-Vayu; Akas-Tejas; Akas-Apas; Akas-Prithivi—and similarly with the other four.

[In other words, in addition to the solar and lunar 'tides' described previously there are tattvic tides, with a major change in the tide every 24 minutes and a minor change every 4 minutes 48 seconds. Starting at sunrise each day the tides run as follows in periods of 4 minutes 48 seconds for a total of two hours:

(1) Akas-Akas	(10) Vayu-Prithivi	(19) Apas-Apas
(2) Akas-Vayu	(11) Tejas-Akas	(20) Apas-Prithivi
(3) Akas-Tejas	(12) Tejas-Vayu	(21) Prithivi-Akas
(4) Akas-Apas	(13) Tejas-Tejas	(22) Prithivi-Vayu
(5) Akas-Prithivi	(14) Tejas-Apas	(23) Prithivi-Tejas
(6) Vayu-Akas	(15) Tejas-Prithivi	(24) Prithivi-Apas
(7) Vayu-Vayu	(16) Apas-Akas	(25) Prithivi-Prithivi
(8) Vayu-Tejas	(17) Apas-Vayu	
(9) Vayu-Apas	(18) Apas-Tejas	

This cycle is repeated every two hours; in effect there are not twenty-five tattvic tides, but fifty. For alternate periods of two hours are under solar and lunar influences—so, for example, a solar Akas-Vayu tattvic tide will be succeeded two hours later by a lunar Akas-Vayu tide.][4]

When the Ida energy—that is, the moon 'breath'—is dominant, says the author of the tantric text,

> it is well to perform the following actions . . . erecting a building . . . going on a distant journey . . . entering a new house . . . marriage . . . taking medicine or tonics . . . seeing a superior . . . amassing of wealth . . . sowing of seed . . . seeing friends . . . going home . . . taking up abode in any village or city . . . and drinking or making water at the time of sorrow, pain, fever etc. . . . During the Tattwas Vayu and Tejas only, are these actions to be done.

[In other words the above actions, and presumably actions of a similar nature, should only be undertaken in the period of 48 minutes commencing 24 minutes after the start of a two-hour period dominated by lunar influences. It is thus clear that even if one accepts the existence of the tattvic tides, and the validity of the above list, it must be interpreted somewhat loosely—obviously one could not complete a journey to a distant place in 48 minutes, nor would it always be convenient to visit friends for so short a time. Either, in these cases, the visit or journey should commence within the 48 minutes period or the list is wholly or partially written in the 'twilight language' and has a secondary meaning.]

When the sun 'breath', that is the subtle energy associated with the Pingala nadi, is dominant the time is favourable for the following actions:

> Reading and teaching hard and difficult subjects of knowledge, sexual intercourse, shipping, hunting, mounting a hill or fort, riding a donkey, camel or horse, swimming over a powerful stream or river, writing, painting, buying and selling, fencing, boxing, seeing a king [sic], bathing, eating, shaving, bleeding—and such like.

[I suspect that this list, like the previous one, must be at least partially written in the twilight language.]

The tantric author then suggests methods by which the adept can supposedly discover which tattvic tide is flowing without engaging in elaborate calculations. He begins by suggesting that one should make

---

4. I have seen a variant of this tattvic tide-table in which the first five sub-tides (i.e. those relating to Akas) as are on p. 82 but the Vayu sub-tides are given as (1) Vayu-Vayu (2) Vayu-Tejas (3) Vayu-Apas (4) Vayu-Prithivi, and, (5) Vayu-Akas. Similar adjustments, which any readers sufficiently interested can work out for themselves, are made to the other three major tides so that each tattvic tide begins with its own sub-tide.

five coloured 'bullets', representing the five tattvas. Then

> . . . let him close his eyes and take one of them out . . . The colour of
> the bullet will be that of the Tattwa then in course . . .

[One could presumably check the accuracy of this indication, which
one would expect to be correct one time in five on a chance basis,
by calculation. It may be that what is being suggested is that when
a particular 'bullet' is chosen the indicated tide is flowing *for the person
who has made the choice*.]⁵

> Actions of a sedate and stable nature . . . to be done when Prithivi the
> Earthly Principle is in course. Those of a fleeting nature . . . are to be
> done during Apas. Those of a hard nature, those in which a man has
> to make violent struggle . . . are to be done during Tejas . . . In the Akasa,
> nothing should be done but meditation, as works begun during this always
> end badly.

[Presumably 'nothing shall be done' means 'nothing should be *begun*
to be done'—one could hardly cease from some hectic activity for 24
minutes in every two-hour period and engage in meditation simply
because one believed the Akas tattvic tide to be flowing.]

> During the day, when the sky is clear, let (the student) . . . for about an
> hour or two withdraw his mind . . . and sitting on an easy chair, let him
> fix his eyes on any particular part of the blue sky, and go on looking at
> it without allowing them to twinkle. At first he will see the waves of the
> water . . . as the eyes become practised, he will see different sorts of buildings
> and so on in the air, and many other wonderful things as well. When
> the Neophyte reaches this stage of practice, he is sure of gaining success.

[This technique is undoubtedly effective if it is persisted with. Whether
the 'wonderful things' seen are projections of some astral or 'tattvic'
reality, or whether they emanate from the Unconscious is, of course,
a matter of opinion. The word 'twinkle' in the above passage should
probably read 'blink'.]

> For the night let the student rise . . . when everything is calm . . . and
> when the calm light of the stars breathe holiness, and a calm rapture enters
> into the soul of man. Let him wash . . . with cold water. Let him put his
> shin bones on the ground, and let the back of his thighs touch his calves,
> and let him put his hands upon his knees, the fingers pointing towards
> the body. Let him now fix his eyes on the tip of his nose . . . he must
> always . . . meditate upon his breath, coming in and going out . . .

---

5. In relation to this see Appendix A for Brodie Innes' remarks on the
subjective elements in the tattvic tides.

[The yogic asana, or posture[6] described above, is extremely simple but produces discomfort, even cramp, after a very short time, in the bodies of most Westerners. With persistence, over a period of weeks or months, it is usually possible to accustom oneself to it. It is simpler, however, to adopt another posture, one in which the body is 'steady and easy'—i.e. the student *forgets* his body.]

by constant practise of this meditation over his breath, the man is to develop two distinct syllables in his thought . . . when a man draws his breath in, a sound is produced which is imitated as 'Han'. When out, the sound 'Sa' . . . the going in and coming out of the breath . . . makes Han-Sa, that is the Name of the Ruler of the Universe . . . At this stage of perfection . . . commence as follows:

Getting up at two or three in the morning and washing himself . . . let him know and fix his mind upon the Tattwa then in course. If the Tattwa then in course be Prithivi let him think of it as . . . having four angles . . . yellow colour, sweet smelling . . . and taking away all diseases. Let him at the same time repeat the word LAM . . .

[This is, of course, mantra yoga; the manuscript goes on to give similar instructions for the other four tattvas—Apas, Tejas, Vayu, and Akasa—the mantras for these being, respectively, VAM, RAM, PAM and HAM.]

By diligent practice . . . these syllables become inseparable from the Tattwas. When he repeats any of these, the special Tattwa appears as he may will . . .

On the Tattwas concludes with some remarks on the connection between the tattvic tides and bodily health and an outline of the way in which the tattvic system can be applied to the 'forecast of futurity'.

Such, then, is the outline of a tantric document which exerted some influence on all the early members of the Golden Dawn, including Crowley, and which has, at least in part, become an integral part of the Western Esoteric Tradition.

There is no doubt, however, that although such men as Brodie Innes and MacGregor Mathers accepted with enthusiasm such tantric teachings and meditations as those outlined above, they would have been horrified by the nature of some of the left-handed tantric rituals which are described in the succeeding chapter.

---

6. Sometimes known as 'The Dragon'. It is perhaps significant that Crowley frequently used this posture.

CHAPTER SIX

Right-Hand Tantra, Left-Hand Tantra

One of the first Portuguese navigators to reach India reported that he had attended the celebration of Mass in an Indian cathedral; 'there were many images of saints', he wrote, 'and some of them had many arms'.

While it seems unlikely that many of the subsequent European visitors to India have been naïve enough to participate in a Hindu rite under the impression that they were celebrating the Christian eucharist, there is no doubt that, until very recent times, the majority of Westerners living in India were remarkably ignorant of the real nature of the very mixed assortment of faiths and cults collectively referred to as Hinduism. Thus, for example, one distinguished nineteenth-century European complained about the noise made by 'Hindoo priests chanting the Koran', while a connection of my own, who spent some months living with the Gosin—ferocious Shiva-worshipping warriors who fought naked saved for sword and cartridge belts—referred to them as 'a sect of Hindoo fakirs'. 'Fakirs' is, of course, a word which can only be applied to Moslems, while a nineteenth-century Brahmin would have been no more likely to recite the Koran than he would to have eaten beef.

Such astounding misconceptions concerning Indian religious life were by no means untypical of nineteenth-century European attitudes, and incomprehension became tinged with horror and disgust as far as Tantra was concerned. Even those rare Europeans who dispassionately reported the supposed facts of left-handed tantric practice were puzzled by its religious aspects. It was not so much that they found it surprising that people should indulge in 'sexual orgies'—indeed, at least one European observer of Tantra was himself rather keen on such enjoyments—but that *they should claim to do so for the purpose of spiritual advancement.*

Thus one Victorian commentator upon Tantra writes of a particular group that they

throw into confusion all the ties of female relationship; natural restraints are wholly disregarded, and a community of women among the votaries inculcated.

On the occasion of the performance of divine worship the women and girls depost their julies . . . in a box in charge of the Guru, or priest. At the close of the rites, the male worshippers take each a julie from the box, and the female to whom it belongs, even were she his sister, becomes his partner for the evening in these lascivious orgies. Yet these Sacteyas (or adorers of Sacti) look upon all but themselves as 'pasu iana', mere brutes![1]

The 'julie' of the above passage is a *choli*, a blouse-like garment, while 'pasu' is at the present day usually transliterated into English as *pashu*, in tantric terminology meaning 'the uninitiated herd'.

Those readers of this book who are acquainted with the history of Gnosticism and European heresy may find the above account of the 'julie road' (*chola-marg*) curiously familiar. It is, in fact, quite remarkably similar to a story which, in various forms, has recurred in a European context for almost two thousand years. In the second century AD the tale was applied to the early Christians:

On the festival they gather with all their children, sisters, mothers, people of both sexes and all ages. When they have feasted, and lasciviousness has been enflamed by drink, meat is thrown to a dog tethered to a lamp. The lamp . . . is overturned and extinguished. Now, in the dark, favourable to shamelessness, they tie the knots of passion, as chance has decided. And so all alike are incestuous, if not in deed at least in complicity . . .

Fifty years or so later Christian writers were attributing similar activities to such Gnostics as the Carpocratians, in the eighth century male initiates of the sect of the Paulicians were accused of incest with their own mothers, and in the eleventh century it was alleged that the dualist Bogomils—the ideological ancestors of the Albigenses—celebrated Easter as follows:

---

1. The author of this disapproving account was a certain Edward Sellon, born at Paddington on 6 January 1818, the son of Edward and Mary Sellon. He was gazetted on 2 February 1834 as an Ensign in the 4th Madras Native Infantry and was retired on pension on 31 May 1846. After his return to England he was for two years, under an assumed name, the driver of the London to Cambridge coach. Subsequently he made his living as a fencing teacher and an author of pornographic novels. He shot himself, in Webbs' Hotel, in April 1866. Sellon's autobiography, *The Ups and Downs of Life*, gives interesting details of the more surprising recreations of a young English officer in the India of the 1830s; his *Annotations on the Sacred Writings of the Hindoos* (a privately printed work heavily plagiarized by Hargrave Jennings in the pages of his *Phallicism*) admirably illustrates just how shocking Tantra was to nineteenth-century Europeans—even to libertines such as Sellon.

In the evening, when the candles are lit, at the time when we celebrate the redemptive Passion of Our Lord, they bring together, in a house chosen for the purpose, girls whom they have initiated into their rites. Then they extinguish the candles, so that the light shall not be witness to their abominable actions, and throw themselves on the girls—each one on whomsoever first falls into his hands, no matter whether she is his sister, his daughter, or his mother.

In the thirteenth century an inquisitor named Conrad of Marburg—who eventually met his downfall when he falsely accused Henry of Sayn of riding upon a gigantic crab—mercilessly executed numerous Rhinelanders whom he believed had indulged in such nocturnal activities, and a century later very similar charges were made against the Waldensians.

Was there then, a European tradition, dating back to the second century, of an erotico-religious rite bearing some resemblance to the *chola-marg* of left-handed Tantra? At first sight it would seem as though an affirmative answer could be given. The fact is, however, that competent historians have examined the truth of all the stories outlined above and have found most of them to be, at best, unproven, and, at worst, totally unfounded. This does not mean, of course, that there is no Western tradition of using the senses, particularly as they relate to physical sexuality, in order to transcend them—but it does mean that group sexuality has been no part of that tradition or, at any rate, has only very recently become part of it.

It might be thought that the same was true of Tantra—i.e. that the report of the *chola-marg* quoted above, and similar reports, are untrue, the fantasies of those who have been outside the tantric tradition and have, either accidentally or deliberately, misinterpreted that tradition.

This is not the case. There is not the slightest doubt that the *chola-marg* has been practised in the past, and is still discreetly practised at the present day, over large parts of northern India, notably Bengal and Rajasthan.

Chola-marg is merely a variant of what is sometimes called *chakra puja*, 'lotus worship', the group sexual activity associated with left-handed Tantra. *Chakra puja* is not in any sense a casual encounter between a number of promiscuous people, a quasi-religious Indian equivalent of a gathering of suburban 'swingers'. On the contrary, it is an act of worship for which the intending participants carefully prepare their bodies and minds by sexual abstinence, meditation, and, on the day immediately preceding the rite, fasting.

After the participants have gathered at the place at which the ceremony is to be held they take hashish or some other preparation derived from *Cannabis indica*, believed to have aphrodisiac effects and, certainly, a mild hallucinogen. While these supposed and certain characteristics of hashish help to make it the 'drug of choice' for practitioners of left-handed Tantra, there seems little reason to doubt that the real reason why tantrics use it as a *preliminary* to rites involving physical sexuality—it is not, it should be noted, a *part* of such rites—is because without it, the overwhelming majority of those brought up within the rigid cultural conventions of Hindu society would be unable, because of psychological inhibitions, to take part in such rites.

This raises the whole question of drug use—whether the drug be illegal, such as LSD, or legal, such as fly agaric—by occultists. In the present century most Western occultists have not only eschewed the use of drugs as a means of 'unloosing the girders of the soul', but have regarded such use as being, quite independently of any legal considerations, dangerous to body, mind, and soul. A minority, however, largely made up of followers of Crowley, have been enthusiastic drug users and, in some cases, abusers. This matter is dealt with at some length in Appendix B of this book; it suffices here to say that any Western occultist who decides to practise left-handed Tantra is unlikely to be so conventional that he or she needs to partake of any chemical substance in order to do so.

The drug taking associated with *chakra puja* is, as said above, a preliminary to the ceremony, not part of it — it is *Vijaya*, 'the giver of victory', which ensures that the participants triumph over the inhibitions which would, for example, prevent them eating beef.

The rite proper begins with the worshippers gathered in a circle, seated on the ground, man alternating with woman, the woman on the *left* of each man being his intended sexual partner—hence, of course, the term left-handed Tantra.

At the centre of the circle stands the male adept who will conduct the ceremony, the 'priest', and near him sits or lies a naked woman, the 'priestess'. For tantrics all women are holy—as one text has it 'every woman is your image, O Shakti, you reside in the forms of all women in this world'—but for the duration of the rite the priestess, the woman at the centre of the circle who is to be the sexual partner of the officiating adept, is considered especially holy, a *particular* manifestation of Shakti. As such her vulva is peculiarly sacred, a symbol of the creative power which sustains the universe, and it is displayed as fully as possible to the assembled congregation, the priestess lying or sitting with her legs held wide apart.

To emphasize that while the ceremony lasts the priestess is not only a manifestation of Shakti in the same way that *all* women are a manifestation of Shakti, but a living incarnation of the Goddess, her body is first ritually cleansed, by being sprinkled with wine and consecrated 'holy water', and then Shakti is invoked into that body by the priest. This latter is done by the priest gently caressing her head, trunk, and limbs while muttering or chanting invocations. Almost every part of the body receives these caresses but particular attention is paid to the vulva, which has an aromatic sandalwood paste applied to it, is lightly kissed, and is then, as the supreme expression of the nature of the Goddess, the recipient of symbolic sacrifice—that is to say libations of water, wine, or coconut milk are poured over it or on the ground beneath it. These libations are, interestingly enough, sometimes poured from a vessel which is shaped something like half a stoned avocado pear and is itself supposedly a symbol of the vulva of the Goddess.

The priestess is now looked upon as being deified, for the time being an avatar of Shakti, and as such she is literally worshipped by the congregation. The woman, as such, is not worshipped—or, at least, not to any greater extent than all women are worshipped—it is the Goddess within her who is the subject of veneration.

As if to emphasize that it is the Goddess who is adored the woman in whom she is incarnated is sometimes of a type regarded as 'worthless' according to the conventional standards of Indian society—for example she will be a member of an untouchable caste, a prostitute, a dancing girl, or even, according to tantric legend, a she-demon.

The ritual worship of the priestess is often immediately followed by her copulation with the priest, the assembled worshippers devoutly observing what is regarded as a sacred action, a physical expression of the eternal embrace of Shiva and Shakti. The sexual coupling is regarded as holy and so are the participants, *but only as manifestations of Shiva and Shakti*. To make apparent that it is Shiva and Shakti who sanctify the rite the priest and priestess are frequently incompatible with one another according to the religious and social laws of orthodox Hinduism. Thus the priestess will perhaps be of a higher caste than the priest, or of a much lower caste, or the wife of another man and thus an adulteress, or even related to the priest in some forbidden degree—perhaps his sister. Such incompatibility is regarded as so much increasing the efficacy of the ritual copulation that the least favourable combination of priest and priestess is regarded as one in which they are legally married to one another.

The congregation now embarks on a feast, a long-drawn-out consumption of the first four of the 'Five Ms'. These are, it will be remembered, *matsya* (fish), *mamsa* (meat, usually beef), *madya* (wine or other alcoholic drink) and *mudra* (supposedly aphrodisiac grains or pulses)—the fifth M is, of course, *maithuna*, ritual sexual coupling.

The word *mudra* has several meanings within the context of left-handed Tantra. Its primary tantric meaning is, as said above, supposedly aphrodisiac substances of vegetable origin; but it is also applied to the female practitioners, usually referred to as Shakta, to the positions that are adopted during intercourse, and to the excitation of the clitoris of the female practitioner by the forefinger of the sadhaka, the male aspirant to tantric illumination. *Mudra* in this last sense is almost invariably an accompaniment to the feast of fish, meat, wine, and *mudra* in its vegetable sense.

When the four Ms have raised the physical and emotional state of the worshippers to the desired pitch—one bordering on erotic and religious frenzy—a general copulation ensues. Throughout this the sadhaka endeavours to think of his partner as not one woman, not even as all women, but as Shakti, the dynamic force which manifests itself in all females. Similarly, the woman, if she is herself a tantric aspirant and not, as is sometimes the case, a prostitute, thinks of her lover as being Shiva.

If this is properly done the orgasm which is the culmination of the rite becomes, so it is claimed, something much more than physical pleasure. The physical orgasm is simultaneously accompanied by a 'spiritual orgasm' in which the eternal duality is transcended and the divine Oneness is experienced. This, strictly speaking, concludes the ceremony, but there is usually a *coda* to the rite. This involves the sadhaka washing the vulva of his partner while she performs a similar service for him. The water that has been used for this purpose is then mingled with water and drunk—a symbolic consumption of the mingled bodies of Shiva and Shakti.

Such *chakra puja* (lotus, or circle, worship) is considered by most left-handed tantrics to be the ideal form in which the Ritual of the Five Ms should be celebrated. However, such collective celebrations would seem to be of comparatively rare occurrence—problems involving secrecy and the general social disapproval of left-handed workings in orthodox Hindu society ensure that most tantrics have to carry out their rites alone save for their partner.

In Buddhist Tantra 'circle worship' is so rare that it almost never takes place, and is certainly not regarded as the ideal norm. Nevertheless, there is a close resemblance between Hindu and Buddhist left-handed workings, and there is only one major difference between them.

That difference is illustrated by a legendary tale concerning Marpa, a Buddhist tantric who flourished at around the same time as the Normans conquered England and was the teacher of Milarepa, perhaps the greatest of Tibetan yogis. Marpa, so it is recounted, wished to ensure that a particular disciple of his should father a 'magical child'—a suitable physical vehicle for the incarnation of a great spiritual teacher. The disciple and his wife were first given an advanced initiation by

Marpa, following which they separately undertook prolonged religious exercises involving ritual, meditation, and invocations of the Bodhisattvas, who were asked to bless the forthcoming magical copulations of the couple.

When these processes had been completed, the couple were the recipients of a further initiation, following which they were led into the sanctum in which Marpa and his consort, the demi-goddess Dagmedma, held court. While these two looked on the disciple and his wife coupled at their feet until the moment of orgasm. At this stage the disciple withdrew from his wife's body and ejaculated into a bowl carved from a human brainpan—a type of container still used in some tantric rituals. Marpa then added certain herbal substances to the contents of the bowl, which were then drunk by the disciple and his wife, the latter becoming pregnant as a result.

The disciple's ingestion of his own semen would seem to have been a symbolic expression of the fact that in left-handed Buddhist Tantra the male practitioner carefully avoids ejaculation. In Hindu left-handed rites exactly the opposite situation prevails, and it is normally considered essential that the male should achieve full orgasm and ejaculation— he 'gives' of himself as fully as possible, and does not try to 'conserve energy' as does the Buddhist practitioner. There are certain exceptions to this, described later, in which the Hindu adept avoids ejaculation.

This divergence is puzzling, but is probably accounted for by a cultural factor, the importance given to the concept of sacrifice (*yajna*) in the *Vedas*. On this level, at least, Hindu tantrics are true to Vedic traditions, and the emission of semen would seem to be regarded as being as truly a sacrifice as the slaying of a goat in honour of Mother Kali.

In Buddhist left-handed Tantra, then, male ejaculation is considered to be undesirable, an unnecessary sacrifice, a loss of the dynamic male energy—the reader will remember the polarity reversal between Buddhist and Hindu Tantra—which physically manifests itself as semen.[2] The Buddhist avoidance of ejaculation, which sometimes takes an extreme form amounting to a virtual obsession, a sort of 'ejaculation phobia', probably accounts for the fact that Buddhist tantrics regard women

---

2. There is, in fact, a tantric Buddhist technique in which ejaculation *does* take place but the semen is then allegedly drawn back into the male body through the urethra. This is believed to happen in the most literal sense; the former Abbot of Kumbum has written that the tantric practitioner may draw back into his body not only the semen he has ejaculated but with it the female ova 'enriching the practitioner . . . the female . . . in turn, may draw into herself something of the male element and transform it . . . into spiritual . . . energy'.

in a way that is markedly different to that which is the norm in Hindu Tantra.

In spite of the fact that India has had a woman Prime Minister there is no doubt that throughout history orthodox Hinduism has held women in comparatively low regard, looking upon them as mere appendages to, first, their fathers, and then their husbands. This has at times led to women being treated as mere chattels—in Rajasthan female infanticide was considered a very minor sin until comparatively recently, while the horrible practice of suttee (a woman burning herself to death on her husband's funeral pyre) was actively encouraged. Womankind was considered to be *spiritually* dangerous; 'There are three kinds of vice', says one medieval Hindu text, 'but the most vicious is womankind; there are seven kinds of poison, but the most poisonous is womankind.' Particularly poisonous, so goes the orthodox argument, is a menstruating woman; she is 'unclean', her breath can poison food, and her husband must avoid sexual relations with her or he too will become defiled, unclean by association.

The point of view adopted by Hindu tantrics, particularly those who use left-handed techniques, is, and has been, radically different from that of orthodoxy. Thus, at the time when orthodoxy regarded suttee as the most virtuous act of which a woman was capable, the author of a tantric text baldly stated that 'That woman who . . . ascends the funeral pyre of her husband goes to hell.' For the devotee of left-handed Tantra women are, quite simply, manifestations of Shakti; to burn them alive, or to encourage them to burn themselves alive, is to sacrilegiously spurn the Goddess.

A similar expression of a belief in the holiness of femininity is to be discerned in the tantric attitude towards menstruation. As far as the adept of left-handed Tantra is concerned a menstruating woman is not unclean but especially holy, and sexual relations with her are not only considered as being permissible, but as intrinsically desirable.

In Buddhist Tantra there are elements of the same sort of veneration of the female principle in general, and female biological functioning in particular; thus some Buddhist texts compare the heavens to the vulva, while elsewhere in such texts it is said that 'Buddhahood resides in the vulva'. But there is also apparent in some texts a fear of the vagina, a dread that this mysterious engine of ecstasy can rob man of his life force by inducing ejaculation. This fear is expressed in strange legends of the *dakini*, she-demons, often of unpleasant aspect, who tempt tantric aspirants into sexual activities culminating in ejaculation and thus, by some process of psychic vampirization, permanently deprives them of their virility.

There is little element of fear of the vagina, terror of feminine vampirism, apparent in those Hindu tantric exercises in which no ejaculation takes place. The motive of such exercises would usually seem to be not the avoidance of ejaculation for its own sake, but the building of a sexual tension—psychic and physical—which will eventually explode in the ecstasy of circle worship or some similar physical expression of the Shiva/Shakti polarity.

A good example of such a non-ejaculatory working—it is so extended that it can hardly be called a rite—is provided by *stri-puja*, 'worship of woman', a technique that, at least on the surface, bears some resemblance to a type of psychological masochism described by such Western sexologists as Havelock Ellis, Magnus Hirschfield, and Norman Haire.

The sadhaka, the male tantric aspirant, begins by becoming the unpaid domestic servant of the woman who, as a manifestation of Shakti, is the object of his worship. For her he performs menial domestic duties, which may include those which would usually be carried out by a sweeper; he is obedient to her every command, regarding the services he renders her as rendered to the Goddess.

At first he sleeps, fully clad, on a mat at the foot of her *charpoy* (stringed bed), ready to be aroused at any time should there be need. After a few weeks he joins her on the *charpoy* but still remains fully clothed.

The next stage is for the sadhaka to unclothe himself at night and lie naked, but still unmoving, beside the body of his mistress. After two weeks of this he begins to use physical caresses. Finally the sadhaka has sexual intercourse with the object of his devotion, but it is *coitus reservatus*, the practice sometimes termed Karezza, in which there is a deliberate avoidance of orgasm and ejaculation.

Such is *stri-puja*, perhaps the oddest of all left-handed techniques.

The rites of right-handed Tantra are precisely the same as those of left-handed Tantra—save that there is a substitution of symbols for reality and that the female partner in the ceremonies and other workings sits on the right hand side of her companion.

Thus, for example, in the ceremony of the Five Ms the symbolic replacements of the authentic Ms might be coconut milk as a substitute for wine, curd cheese for beef, candied ginger for fish, rice or dhal for the aphrodisiac mudra, and a chaste kiss—or even a gift of flowers—for copulation. Even practitioners of right-handed Tantra admit that this 'path of substitution' is a more difficult one to follow than left-handed Tantra. Quite apart from the fact that most people find it difficult to raise themselves to the verge of the ecstasy of the embrace of Shakti or Shiva at a feast of coconut milk, curd cheese, and boiled rice, the absence of cultural and psychic shock as an element in right-handed workings would seem to be decidedly disadvantageous—as explained on page 14 there is an element of 'psychic shock therapy' in many systems of occult and mystical training and this is very notable in left-handed Tantra.

The phrase 'left-handed' in relation to Tantra of a type involving physical sexuality is an unfortunate one in an occidental context; it is very easy for a European or North American to make the false verbal transition from 'left', via 'sinister', to 'evil'. Those who have made such a transition have often been led into a serious misunderstanding of the historical development of tantric techniques, assuming that right-handed Tantra is 'authentic' and 'pure', the 'real Tantra' of which left-handed Tantra is some sort of illegitimate derivation. Some, who have included distinguished members of the Theosophical Society, have even gone so far as to regard left-handed Tantra as a form of black magic, bearing the same relationship to 'real Tantra' as does the legendary 'Mass of St Sécaire' (according to Breton folklore a requiem mass said for a living person with the object of causing that person's death) to an orthodox Mass.

Such beliefs are against all the historical evidence. Not only do left-handed techniques predate the 'substitute worship' of right-handed Tantra, *but the polarity theories which are accepted by all schools of Tantra seem to have been derived from occult rites and exercises involving physical sexuality.* In other words, the methods employed by practitioners of left-handed Tantra have not been invented as the result of deliberate or accidental misunderstandings of some 'pure' tantric theory. On the contrary, tantric theory has come into existence as the result of efforts to draw some sorts of philosophical/cosmological conclusions which would satisfactorily explain the *results* of left-handed tantric practice.

This is not to say, of course, that there have never been cults derived from left-handed Tantra which can be regarded as analogous to the black magic of Western tradition. There is, in fact, evidence that such cults have existed in the past, and that some of them still exist at the present day.

Characteristically such cults have exhibited an obsession with death, and have celebrated rites which combine such elements as coprophagy, anthropophagy, and abnormal sexual practices. One such ceremony, which, according to rumour, is still performed in great secrecy in parts of Rajasthan, is an unorthodox version of the Ceremony of the Five Ms in which the substances used are *mutra*, human urine, *mala*, human faeces, *medha*, human blood, *mah-mamsa*, human flesh, and *mehana*, penis, which in this context, so it is said, is interpreted as buggery.

Whether such rites do, in fact, still take place is uncertain. People tend to attribute all sorts of amazingly unpleasant activities to the members of secret religious groups, and just as in medieval Europe the harmless Waldenses were believed to indulge in incest, murder, and the worship of Satan, so in northern India at the present day left-handed tantrics are sometimes alleged to carry out ceremonies involving human sacrifice and cannibalism.

But while many of such allegations can probably be safely dismissed as malicious fantasy there can be no doubt that they are based on a substratum of reality. Certain sects which can be regarded as having a tantric derivation, or, at any rate, having been influenced by Tantra, have in the past practised murder on a very large scale. The most notable of these was the notorious robber-cult of the *phansigars*, 'deceivers', the Thugs, who adored Kali as an incarnation of Shakti, celebrated rites with a worship in which those who tasted a consecrated coarse sugar believed they experienced 'the embrace of Kali', engaged in ritual strangulation of those whom they robbed. Undoubtedly of tantric origin were the Kapilakas (worshippers of Chamunda, another avatar of Shakti) who still survive at the present day and in the past certainly practised both necrophilia and human sacrifice—a treatise held in high regard by some members of this cult proclaims that 'by the sacrifice of three men the Goddess is happy for a *lakh* of years'.

It might be thought that such bloodiness would be alien to the gentle philosophy of the Buddha, but similar death-orientated derivatives of Tantra seem to have been widely practised in pre-communist Tibet.

Some of these cults undoubtedly practised human sacrifice, a feature of the shamanistic Bon religion which dominated Tibet until its population was largely converted to Buddhism in the ninth century. There is little doubt that there has been a considerable cultural cross-fertilization between Tantra and Bon, and it seems likely that at least some of the more death-obsessed Buddhist tantric cults adapted Bon techniques to their own purposes. Possibly the tantric Chod ceremony illustrates such a Bon influence upon Buddhist tantra—certainly the adept who performs this ceremony has to behave much more like a Central Asian shaman than a Buddhist monk.

'Chod' is derived from a Tibetan word meaning 'to cut, to dismember'. Its use as a descriptive word for the rite in question arises from the fact that the most common method of disposing of the dead in Tibet is to cut them into small pieces, expose them in a place set apart for that purpose, and leave them to be consumed by carrion-eating birds.

A very full account of the Chod rite is to be found in the pages of *Tibetan Yoga and Secret Doctrines* (OUP, 1935), which was edited by Dr Y. W. Evan-Wentz, who seems to have found tantric ceremonies involving death less offensive than those involving sexuality. It suffices here to say that the adept uses visualization techniques (of a very similar type to those employed, for very different purposes, by the Adepti of the Golden Dawn) in order to imagine his own extinction. During the course of the rite, which usually takes place on the site of a 'dismemberment ground' littered with bones and pieces of decaying flesh, the adept *dances* while conceiving of himself as a living corpse, dead, but paradoxically, still conscious of everything which happens. He endeavours to feel his body being beheaded, dismembered and fed, not to wild beasts and birds, but to the terrifying demons of Tibetan legend.

No one who has not undertaken the Chod working can know what the practitioner actually experiences on the psychic level of creative imagination. But it is worth reporting that those who have undertaken such workings claim that they have *physically* felt the pangs of death, the pain inflicted by the corpse-dismemberer's knife, and the agony of being eaten and digested by demons. Whether or not this is so, there can be no doubt of the supposed function of the Chod rite—the induction of a spiritual rebirth. However ghastly the imagery of the Chod rite and the surroundings in which it normally takes place, it is, in essence, identical with all the great rites of initiation; a man or woman is slain and reborn to a new life. The Chod practitioner dances, festooned with bones and wearing a cap and apron tailored from tanned human skin, amidst corpses; but, at root, he is undergoing precisely the same psychic experiences as are intended to be induced by all initiations concerned with a symbolic death and resurrection of the candidate—whether that enacted 'death' is that of some legendary builder, or of some mysterious 'Father C.R.C.', or whether it is, as in some tantric cults, the 'little death' of the orgasm.

The Chod rite can, I think, be regarded as a legitimate extension of the techniques of left-handed Tantra—but, of course, only in the peculiar cultural milieu of Tibet.[3] For any non-Tibetan to engage in physical activities even remotely resembling those which are integral to the Chod rite would be both pointless and clear evidence of psychic pathology. Even in pre-communist Tibet those who had taken this path were often regarded with much suspicion, not only by the general population, but by those who were themselves tantrics. It seemed only a small step from the Chod rite to the outright sorcery and necromancy of the Dug-pa cult, whose initiates were alleged to engage in practices including a mode of divination involving the reanimation of the dead,

---

3. There is some reason to think that the Chod ceremony may be a tantric Buddhist development of a primitive shamanistic rite involving real or illusory *physical* self-mutilation; see Appendix C for a description of what may be a proto-Chod working.

necrophilia, and the kidnapping of young girls for the purpose of using them in rites involving sex magic.

It must be emphasized that the employment of the Chod rite, still more the use of the techniques supposedly characterizing the Dug-pa sect, have always been confined to a very small minority of Tibetan mystics and magicians. The average Tibetan, whether peasant or monk, has never wanted any direct dealings with the demon princes and princesses whose terrifying images are portrayed in the holy of holies of all Tibetan monasteries, even those of the gentle Yellow Hat sect.

In fact Tantra, which has always been closely associated with Tibetan Buddhism since the time of Padmasambhava (who flourished in the eighth century and was the founder and 'Precious Teacher' of the Red Hat sect)[4] has usually been vaguely regarded as 'foreign' by most Tibetans. This is, perhaps, a folk memory of the time, more than a thousand years ago, when native Bon shamans and tantric Buddhist missionaries from India and the semi-mythical kingdom of Urgyan fought for the soul of the Tibetan people.

In spite of the suspicion with which ordinary Tibetans have looked upon Tantra, there is no doubt that many of its methods have become deeply embodied in Tibetan Buddhism and Bon—so deeply embodied, in fact, that it has been forgotten that such methods are, in origin, tantric. Thus there is no real doubt that almost all the physical and meditative techniques collectively known as 'Tibetan yoga' are derived from the Buddhist Tantra which flourished in northern India a millennium and more ago.

Tibetan yoga, like that of Hindu Tantra, is concerned with the vivification of psychic centres and is, in essence, identical with the whole body of techniques concerned with arousing the serpent power of the sleeping Kundalini. The only real difference is that the Tibetan yogi is less concerned with elaborate theories of esoteric physiology involving thousands of chakras and nadis than is the Hindu tantric. The Buddhist tantric is not particularly interested in the exact nature of the physical analogues of psychic centres, or in conceiving of such centres as positioned in ways precisely aligned with the organs of the physical

---

4. Padmasambhava, called by Tibetans Lopon Rinpoche, was born in the mysterious tantric kingdom of Urgyan, which seems to have been somewhere between Afghanistan and Kashmir. According to legend his origins were miraculous, and he was said to have appeared from inside an enormous lotus bud. It seems more likely that he was related in some way to the Royal House of Urgyan. What is beyond question is that he was a tantric, as is indicated by the legend that he received secret initiations from 'the Goddessess who dwell in graveyards'.

body—in a sense he 'makes' his chakras, and thinks of them as positioned wherever it suits him to have them positioned.

The central element of the Buddhist tantric yoga of Tibet is a complex series of visualization exercises. In these so-called 'tantric art' is of great importance—the erotic images of Tantra, sculpted or painted, are not just intended to be looked at, they are intended to be *used*. The tantric aspirant looks at such an image, recreates it in his own mind, seeing it first 'as through a glass darkly' and then with terrifying clarity. This stage achieved, which sometimes takes many years of unremitting concentration and visualization, the aspirant endeavours to identify himself with the god or goddess which he or she has, in a sense, created. When such an identification is complete, yogis endeavour to dissolve the visualized images and, consequently, themselves and 'enter the Void'—a curious term which, so it is to be presumed, can only be really meaningful to those who have experienced 'the great Void'.

There are a number of 'schools' of such Tibetan tantric yoga, of which the best known is that of Naropa, an eleventh-century tantric saint who, according to legend, had achieved illumination as a result of his mystic sexual encounter with a dakini—a strange demoness combining the attributes of a succubus, a harpy, an initiatrix, and a psychopomp—who manifested herself to him as 'a leprous old crone'.

There are six branches of Naropean tantric yoga. They are:

(1) The yoga of bodily fire
(2) The yoga of the astral body
(3) The yoga of the dream state
(4) The yoga of the intermediary state
(5) The yoga of mind transference
(6) The yoga of the Clear Light.

Many of these varieties of Naropean yoga are allegedly productive of extraordinary physical phenomena, some of which seem reasonably well authenticated. Thus, for example, there are reports of practitioners of the yoga of bodily fire (whose visualization techniques include imagining oil dripping from a psychic centre in the head to a 'fire' burning in the region of the solar plexus) sitting naked amidst the Tibetan snows and drying wet sheets wrapped around their bodies.

If such phenomena do take place they are, of course, only side-effects such as are supposedly associated with all schools of tantric 'form yoga'[5] and their real purpose, as has been said, is the achievement of the Void.

---

5. The term 'form yoga' is applied to those schools of tantric yoga in which forms are visualized. There is also a 'formless' tantric yoga, which is looked upon as being less psychically dangerous than form yoga, but lacking the spiritual 'kick', the ability to *throw* the adept into the Void, of the latter.

While the terminology differs the same is true of Layayoga of India, which, it will be remembered, is concerned with arousing the Kundalini, the sleeping Shakti, into activity, inducing it to rise through the chakras, successively vivifying each one, and, finally, have it unite, in the psychic centre termed the *Sahasrara*, in blissful marriage with Shiva.

Layayoga is today so widely practised by men and women who do not use any other tantric techniques and, indeed, might well regard with horror at least some of those techniques, that it is sometimes forgotten that not only does Layayoga have its origins in Tantra, but that *it only makes sense in terms of Shiva/Shakti polarity theory.*

The serpent power of the sleeping Kundalini is no more and no less than a particular manifestation of Shakti in the individual human being; it is not the *only* such manifestation—as far as tantric polarity theory is concerned, every aspect of the body, mind, and psyche of each and every human being is an expression of the Shiva/Shakti embrace which creates and sustains the totality of things.

In the same way the individual Shiva dwelling in the *Sahasrara* chakra is only a particular manifestation of all the Shiva aspects of the totality, and the Shiva/Shakti orgasm which results from the Shakti power of the Kundalini arising and mating with Shiva is, like the result of a successful performance of the Ritual of the Five Ms, a particular manifestation of the everlasting orgasm of the static/dynamic polarity.

That this is so does not in any way devalue the subjective (in a sense) marriage of Shiva and Shakti in the individual human being. Accounts given by those who have experienced this marriage make it clear that it is, for them at least, the supreme experience which can be undergone by an individual human being. Thus, for example, in his book *Kundalini* (1971) Gopi Krishna described how he experienced 'an effulgent, cascading shower of brilliant vital energy . . . filling my head with a blissful lustre'.

As will be shown in the next chapter there are Western occult techniques which are, in essence, almost identical with those employed by practitioners of Layayoga for the purpose of arousing the serpent power.

CHAPTER SEVEN

The Middle Pillar and The Serpent Power

There is an occult visualization exercise, widely used by Western occultists, which is known in one esoteric group, allegedly Druidic in origin but at one time led by an initiate of the Golden Dawn, as 'the construction of the illuminated spine'. At least some readers of this book will know of it under the more widely used term 'the Exercise of the Middle Pillar' and will be aware that it is concerned with subjective aspects of the qabalistic Tree of Life.

The nature of this exercise is described in the following document, a short didactic treatise which was circulated amongst initiates of the Golden Dawn offshoot known as the Stella Matutina, 'the Morning Star'.

In the aura which interpenetrates and surrounds our physical bodies, we are to build up a replica of the Tree of Life. The Pillar of Severity is on our right side, the Pillar of Mercy is on our left, and the Pillar of Equilibrium in our midst.

It is best to build up the Middle Pillar first. To do this stand up and raise yourself in imagination to your Kether—a brilliant light above your head. Imagine this light descending to Daath, at the nape of your neck, and thence to Tiphereth in the heart where it glows like sunlight and whence it radiates into the other sephiroth.

From Tiphereth the light goes to Yesod in the region of the hips [this is clearly a euphemism: for hips read genitals], and thence to Malkuth in which your feet are planted. Having made a clear image of the Middle Pillar, you can then establish the other sephiroth by vibrating the Deity Names . . .

1. Imagine yourself standing in the Temple, facing west. The Black Pillar of Severity will be on your right, the White Pillar of Mercy on your left.

2. Imagine now that the Black Pillar is reflected on your right side, the White Pillar on your left.

3. Take a deep breath and raise your consciousness to your Kether above your head and vibrate the name AHIH—which means I AM. Imagine the Light flowing down through Daath (at the nape of your neck) to Tiphereth.

4. In the same manner, establish Yesod in the name SHADDAI EL CHAI—which means ALMIGHTY LIVING GOD—and Malkuth in the name ADONAI HA-ARETZ—which means LORD OF THE KINGDOMS OF EARTH.

5. Make the Qabalistic Cross to indicate that you have called down the Light of your Kether and balanced it in your aura. Then let the imagination dwell on the aura and see it oval and clear, pulsating with the glow from Tiphereth.

If you are called to see anyone who is ill, who is depressed, or who has a depressing effect on you, you should do this exercise beforehand. In the case of the person who has a depressing effect upon you, you may also imagine that your aura is hardened at the edge so that they are unable to penetrate it and so deplete your vitality—which is generally what such sensations mean.

In all these practices it is well to remember that Strength is in Silence. If you talk about them . . . or if you try to analyse their effect, you will not benefit by them. Try them with simple faith and in silence for a year . . .

It is better at first to keep your aura to yourself, rather than to try to flow out towards others. Unless you are particularly vital and well-balanced, you will only waste energy . . . modes of healing . . . should be eschewed for a time.

The subjective sephiroth referred to above (e.g. as 'your Kether') are, of course, the microcosmic equivalents of the 'objective sephiroth' described on pages 38-39. The black and white pillars referred to in the instruction are those used in the Neophyte ritual of the Golden Dawn and its successors, and the fact that those using the exercise are instructed to imagine themselves 'facing West' merely means that the qabalistic Tree of Life when applied to the human form is reversed, as in a mirror. In other words, those sephiroth which appear on the *left* in the usual diagrammatic representation of the Tree of Life are visualized as being on the *right* side of the human form and vice versa—it is rather as though the Tree is conceived of as being slightly taller than a particular human being and then that person stands with his back to the Tree. 'Vibrate the name AHIH', and similar instructions, refer to a technique which is described in a Golden Dawn document entitled *Flying Roll XII.*[1]

The Operator should first of all rise as high as possible towards the Divine White Brilliance in Kether—keeping the mind raised to the plane of loftiest aspiration . . . The ordinary mode of vibrating is as follows. Take a deep and

---

1. Some of the Golden Dawn instructional manuscripts known as Flying Rolls are to be found in volumes three and four of Israel Regardie's *Golden Dawn.* The rest, including the 'fugitive Flying Rolls' discovered by Mr R. A. Gilbert, will be found in *Astral Projection, Ritual Magic and Alchemy* by S. L. MacGregor Mathers and Others (which will shortly be published by The Aquarian Press).

full breath and concentrate your consciousness in your heart . . . you should endeavour to bring down the While Brilliance into your heart, prior to centreing your consciousness there.

Then formulate the letters of the Name required in your heart, in white, and feel them written there. Be sure to formulate the letters in brilliant white light . . . Then, emitting the breath slowly pronounce the letters so that the sound vibrates within you, and imagine that the breath, while quitting the body, swells you . . . Pronounce the Name as if you were vibrating it through the whole Universe, and as if it did not stop until it reached the further limits.

It will be obvious to readers that this simple—perhaps deceptively simple—exercise bears at least some resemblance to the tantric process of raising the Kundalini. There is the same emphasis on vivifying psychic centres (and it does not matter whether those centres are called 'chakras' or 'sephiroth on the replica of the Tree of Life built up in the aura') and the essence of the two processes is the setting up of a flow of energy through the centre of the 'subtle body'.

There is, however, one very important difference between the two processes. In one, the tantric technique of Layayoga, the energy flow is upward towards the psychic centre which is visualized as being above the crown of the head. In the others, the Middle Pillar Exercise, the flow is exactly reversed, the visualized energy current flowing downwards from the subjective Kether, also conceived of as being above the head.

Before considering these similarities and differences in more detail it is worth saying something about the origins and development of the Middle Pillar Exercise.

The instructional document regarding this exercise which, in slightly abbreviated form, I have reproduced above dates from a fairly late stage in the history of the Golden Dawn and its successor orders. It was an official instruction of the Portal grade of the Stella Matutina and, in the form I have given it, was probably not compiled before c.1910.

Nevertheless, it can be considered as authentically relating to the Golden Dawn tradition as it is merely a simplification, codification, and application of certain teachings which were current in the Order well before 1900, the year in which the Golden Dawn split into competing and hostile factions.

The teachings in question are scattered throughout various documents circulated amongst initiates of the sub-grade of Zelator Adeptus Minor, and of these, two are of particular importance. The first is entitled *Lecture on Man the Microcosm*. In this it is taught that the subtle body of a human being must be considered as taking the shape of a sphere, the 'Sphere of Sensation' or 'the Magical Mirror'. This sphere is described as 'an imitation or copy of the Sphere of the Universe'—this is, of course, only another way of expressing the general idea, common to Tantra and Western occultism, that man the microcosm is a 'miniature edition' of the macrocosm, the totality of things. In the sphere of the subtle body, says the *Lecture*, 'Man is placed between four pillars of the Tree of Life as projected in a sphere.'

The reference to the *four* pillars of the Tree of Life is explained in the second of the documents mentioned above, part of an 'Abstract of the Tarot' entitled *The Tree of Life As Projected In a Solid Sphere*. This is primarily concerned with the astrological concept of the sphere of the heavens, as shown in a celestial globe, but it is equally applicable to the psychic sphere, the subtle body of a human being. The document explains that the Middle Pillar of the Tree of Life 'will form the invisible Axis of the Sphere, the Central point corresponding to Tiphereth. This latter Sephirah together with that of Yesod will be completely hidden from view [this will not, of course, apply to Kether and Malkuth, the 'poles' of the Sphere of Sensation, which will be at the outer surface of the sphere] so that Tiphereth will be at the exact centre of the Sphere.'

In terms of the subjective Tree of Life, in which, as explained on page 71, the sephiroth of the Middle Pillar correlate with the seven chakras of tantric esoteric physiology, it is apparent that the north pole of the Sphere will be Kether, the Sahasrara chakra, which corresponds to a position slightly above the crown of the head. Similarly, the centre of the subjective Sphere will be Tiphereth, the Anahata chakra.

One of the tasks of the Theoricus Adeptus Minor of the Golden Dawn was to establish the Tree of Life in his or her own subtle body—the concept of doing this bears some resemblance to the Buddhist tantric idea (described in the previous chapter) that the aspirant in a sense *constructs* his own chakras. So important was this interior work considered by the pre-1900 initiates of the Golden Dawn that one group of them who participated in joint magical workings—a sort of secret society within a secret society—called themselves The Sphere.

In view of all the above it is apparent that the 'simple' Stella Matutina technique described at the beginning of this chapter, the Middle Pillar Exercise, is the establishment of the central axis of the Sphere of Sensation, with Kether as its north pole, Malkuth as its south.

In attempting to correlate the Middle Pillar Exercise with the tantric techniques associated with the arousal of the Kundalini and the vivification of the chakras a very important point arises in connection with Malkuth, the south pole of the posited Sphere of Sensation.

While this Sphere pertains to other modes of being than the material world of atoms and molecules, and therefore has no physical, three-dimensional location, the tradition is that it does, in a sense, have analogues in the ordinary world of space-time. It supposedly corresponds to a sphere, a sort of psychic bubble, surrounding the physical body, and, according to the teaching given in the Golden Dawn documents quoted earlier, the north pole of the Sphere is above the crown of the head and its centre is in a position corresponding to the human heart. Where, then, is its south pole, the Malkuth of the microcosmic Tree of Life?

According to various Golden Dawn instructional documents it is 'where your feet are planted'. On a purely symbolic basis this seems satisfactory enough; Malkuth represents 'dense earth' and the latter is clearly that on which one stands. But it is a curiously shaped Sphere which, in human terms, has its north pole above the crown of the head, its south pole below the feet, and its centres at the level of the heart. It would seem that once again, as in the comparisons between the chakras and the Tree of Life such as that made by Dion Fortune, the qabalists of the Western Esoteric Tradition have been led astray by a crude comparison of human physiology with the Tree of Life. It is clear that in a sphere with its centre in about the region of the heart and its north pole slightly above the crown of the head, the south pole must be in the region of what the compiler of the Stella Matutina document coyly called 'the nips'—i.e. the genitals and perineum. This strongly supports the equation between Malkuth subsumed by Yesod and the Muladhara chakra made in an earlier chapter.

The skeletonic form of the Middle Pillar Exercise—a visualization of the 'Divine White Brilliance' of the subjective Kether (which is precisely the same thing, so it would seem, as the Sahasrara chakra) flowing down through Daath, Tiphereth and Yesod and earthing itself in Malkuth— can be built up into a complex visualization exercise which, so it is claimed, charges the practitioner with a glowing vibrant energy.

When done in this way the exercise usually begins with the operator performing the simple gestures referred to as the Lesser Banishing Ritual of the Pentagram. This is by no means essential but it is believed to 'clear the psychic air'; i.e. it is a ritual separation of the operator's mind from the cares and pleasures of everyday life and thus helps to induce a mood in which the exercise can more easily be carried out.

The Middle Pillar Exercise is then carried out in precisely the same way as outlined in the document quoted on p. 101 but, in addition, certain visualizations, comparable to those carried out by the tantric yogis of Tibet, accompany its performance. These visualizations can be extremely complex, involving the building up, in accordance with very precisely defined rules, of the images of various 'archangels'. In their simplest form, however, these exercises are largely concerned with the psychic effects on the subjective sephiroth, the chakras, of colour.

The operator visualizes the 'Divine White Brilliance' of Kether flowing into Daath, at the nape of the neck, and forming a whirling lavender blue circle; from there the Kether-energy is visualized as flowing into Tiphereth, at the region of the heart, forming a whirling gold circle; the energy is then conceived of as flowing into Yesod—a whirling purple circle—and from thence to Malkuth. Strictly speaking the colours of the latter are citrine, olive, russet and black (the Malkuth circle is quartered), but the difficulties of visualizing a whirling, four-coloured circle are so immense that Malkuth is best imagined as being a very dark green approaching black. Theoretically there is no reason why the practitioner should not visualize the various chakras/sephiroth as being as large as soup plates or as small as pinheads; in practice it is usually considered most convenient to imagine them as being about four inches in diameter.

The Middle Pillar Exercise is a sort of Kundalini yoga in reverse. In the latter the serpent power is awakened from its sleep 'at the base of the spine', i.e. the Muladhara chakra, and rises through, successively, the Svadisthana, Manipura, Anahata, Vishuddha, and Ajna chakras until, finally, it reaches the Sahasrara chakra where the Shiva/Shakti marriage takes place.

In the Middle Pillar Exercise the energy flow is downwards from the Sahasrara chakra (Kether) to the Ajna and Vishuddha chakras (Daath as the focus of Chokmah and Binah, see p. 72), to the Manipura and Anahata chakras (Tiphereth), to the Svadisthana chakra (Yesod as the focus of the astral triangle), and to the Muladhara chakra (Yesod proper). Finally the energy flow is earthed in Malkuth.

Many initiates of the Stella Matutina seem to have been well aware of the 'correspondence-in-reverse' between the Exercise of the Middle Pillar and the tantric process of Kundalini arousal. Thus the late Dr Francis Israel Regardie, at one time Aleister Crowley's secretary but subsequently an initiate of the Stella Matutina, argued that the two processes are only distinguished from one another by one thing, this being that the Middle Pillar Exercise reflects a Western concern with the world of matter and its practicalities, with 'bringing the Divine down into humanity' and spiritualizing the physical, while Kundalini yoga is 'otherworldly', rejects material things and is concerned with divorcing the soul from the flesh and uniting it with the Absolute.[2]

With the greatest respect for the memory of Dr Regardie and the many excellent books he wrote—books for which all students of the

---

2. See the various editions of Dr Regardie's excellent book *The Middle Pillar*. It is also worth referring to the same writer's *Art of True Healing*, in which an attempt is made to apply the Middle Pillar techniques to the restoration of the physical and psychic health of others, and to his *Foundations of Practical Magic* (Aquarian Press, 1979, 1982).

Golden Dawn magical system owe an enormous debt of gratitude to their author—I think he was mistaken on this matter.

It seems to me that he disregarded the fact that in the Middle Pillar Exercise, however successfully it may be performed and of whatever desirable results it may be productive, *there is no explosive marriage of polarities*. It is true that the energy of the Sahasrara/Kether chakra is transmitted 'downwards' with the object of giving life and power to the other chakras, but there is no transference of *essence*, the inmost being, of the subjective Kether (Shiva, in tantric terminology) to the 'site' of the subjective Yesod, the Muladhara chakra where dwells the serpent power. Nor, of course, is there an 'upward' transference from Yesod to Kether, from the Muladhara to the Sahasrara. And without such a transference of one sort or the other the marriage of opposites cannot be consummated.

To say this is not in any way to consider the Middle Pillar Exercise valueless or intrinsically inferior to the processes employed in arousing the Kundalini. On the contrary, for the purposes for which it is intended most of those who have used it over an extended period of time have found it extremely effective. But those purposes are not the same as those of Kundalini yoga which, in the final analysis, has exactly the same purpose as all tantric rituals—the slaying of opposites in the blissful copulation of Shiva and Shakti.

Nevertheless, as is explained in the following chapter, the adaptation of the occidental exercise of the Middle Pillar to tantric purposes is perfectly feasible—the tantric Way of Action in the context of the techniques associated with the Western Esoteric Tradition.

CHAPTER EIGHT

Tantric Techniques of Yoga and Meditation For Westerners

It is sometimes claimed that it is possible to practise Tantra without being aware that one is doing so. Tantra, so it is said, is the natural religion of the Black aeon, the 'Kali yuga', in which we live, and at the present day the 'vibes' of Tantra are, in the words of Benjamin Walker, 'in the air, to be picked up by anyone ready to receive them'.

Perhaps this is so, but one must beware of assuming that anyone who shows a disregard for the social attitudes of the society in which he or she lives is a 'natural tantric', a sort of holy fool who has achieved, or is in the process of achieving, that liberation which is the goal of Tantra. The plain facts are that most fools are no more than fools, most libertines no more than libertines. The authors of ancient tantric texts were well aware of this. In the words of one such writer:

If perfection be attained by drinking wine, then every drunkard is a saint. If virtue consists of eating meat, then every carnivorous animal in the world is virtuous. If eternal happiness derives from copulation, then all beings will be eternally happy . . . Those who use Kaula worship [i.e. the five Ms] but are of other sects [i.e. have no real belief in Tantra] shall be doomed to as many incarnations as there are hairs on the body of a man.

Clearly one must not assume that all those Westerners who, over the last forty years, have rejected the sexual and social mores of occidental culture—the beat poets, the hippy advocates of allegedly 'mind-expanding' drugs, bisexual rock stars, and so on—have been engaged, whether they knew it or not, in the practice of the techniques of Tantra. One must adopt a suspicious attitude towards all claims of this sort. One judges the quality of a tree by its fruit, and one should judge supposed mystics by a similar criterion. To me, at least, much of the fruit produced by the 'natural tantrics' seems rotten ripe, no part of a healthy diet.

A similar attitude of suspicion should characterize the would-be

TANTRIC TECHNIQUES OF YOGA AND MEDITATION   109

tantric's examination of his own motives. This is particularly the case when such aspirants are attracted to left-handed Tantra—especially to a sort of 'formless Tantra' which some Westerners claim to practise and which seems to consist of no more than averrring a religious motive for over-eating, over-drinking, and engaging in sexual athletics.

One way in which one can distinguish the real from the false tantric is that the former will usually have engaged in much meditation and visualization—both very hard work if properly performed—before engaging in ritual workings of left- or right-handed varieties.

Pranayama—breath control exercises—are almost always both a preliminary and an accompaniment to such interior meditative work, and the Western occultist who wishes to commence a serious enquiry into the efficacy of tantric techniques should begin his or her investigations by some months of pranayama.

There are numerous books and pamphlets dealing with pranayama and the aspirant can, if he or she wishes, purchase one of these and faithfully follow the techniques it lays down. But here a word of warning is necessary: there is no occult technique about which more claptrap has been written than pranayama. Not only has it been asserted that pranayama cures all the ills to which the flesh is heir, from halitosis to fallen arches, from insomnia to obesity, but it has been claimed that through the regular employment of pranayama the human lifespan can be extended to over two hundred years. In reality there is no evidence whatsoever that practitioners of pranayama are any healthier than a person who gets his exercise by such unoccult pursuits as walking, canoeing, or even practising the national indoor pastime. There is, in fact, some evidence that pranayama may be positively damaging to the health of some people suffering from asthma and certain respiratory diseases, and anyone who feels any doubts concerning their own respiratory health would be well advised to seek medical approval before embarking on the more complex varieties of pranayama; and everyone, regardless of their state of health, should avoid following the advice, given in more than one book on pranayama, to persist in certain advanced exercises until acute chest pains are experienced.

Most Western occultists who have employed pranayama as part of a regime of 'psychic athletics' have found it best to start with the following simple exercise:

Find a posture which is steady and easy, i.e. one in which one is as little conscious of bodily stresses and strains as is possible. The exact posture adopted will vary from one individual to another, but the yogic asana sometimes referred to as 'the god' is probably the most comfortable for the majority of Westerners. The position is that in which the gods of ancient Egypt were often portrayed—sitting on a chair, back and head fully erect, knees together with hands resting lightly upon them. A good alternative is the so-called Dragon asana, described on page 85. Then, when a posture has been attained, perhaps by a process of trial and error, which can be comfortably maintained for a period of ten or fifteen minutes, begin daily, or twice daily, deep breathing exercises. Each session should last for a minimum of ten minutes.

Simply breathe in slowly and deeply, completely filling the lungs, and then breathing out even more slowly. Ideally the latter process should take twice as long as the former, but it is usually some time before the experimenter reaches this stage—weeks or, in some cases, months of regular daily exercise.

It is usual, although not essential, to accompany the act of inspiration with the mental repetition of the phrase 'the breath flows in', and that of expiration with the phrase 'the breath flows out'. More important, so it is claimed, is the visualization of a stream of brilliant white energy entering the lungs and flooding the body with each breath.

When this simple exercise has been mastered the experimenter goes on to pranayama proper—that is to say, exercises in which the practitioner not only breathes in (purak) and out (rechack) but for a time does neither—a period referred to as kumbhak.

Kumbhak, the intervals of inactivity, can be between breaths, i.e. with the lungs empty, or in the midst of a breathing cycle, i.e. with the lungs full. So there can be either a threefold pranayama cycle—inhalation, retention, exhalation—or a fourfold cycle of inhalation, retention, exhalation, and inaction with lungs emptied.

A simple form of this fourfold cycle was part of the prescribed meditative work of newly admitted members of the Neophyte grade of the Golden Dawn and in the relevant instructional document the practitioner was instructed to:

1. Empty the lungs and remain thus while counting four.
2. Inhale, to the count of four, feeling yourself filled with breath to the throat.
3. Hold this breath while counting four.
4. Exhale, counting four until the lungs are empty.

This should be practised, counting slowly or quickly, until you obtain a rhythm that suits you—one that is comforting and stilling. Having attained this, count the breath thus for two or three minutes, until you feel quiet, and then proceed with the meditation.

As will be clear from the above, the main purpose of this exercise was the stilling of mind and body as a preliminary to meditation, not the practising of pranayama for its own sake, still less as a first step in tantric visualization processes.

Those who undertake the practice for the latter purpose should extend the 'two or three minutes' mentioned in the instruction to, firstly, five minutes, then ten or fifteen minutes, and, finally twenty minutes. In theory the latter period can be greatly exceeded, but most Western practitioners seem to find this counter-productive, becoming excessively conscious of their bodies and physical surroundings—to sit still, doing nothing but breathing, for extended periods is much more difficult than might be thought.

The 'counting to four' technique of timing the phases of the cycle is traditional but rough-and-ready. There is a tendency to imperceptibly speed up or slow down the count which, over a few minutes, results in radical change in the length of the cycle; after ten minutes an observer equipped with a stop-watch will note that the length of a full cycle will be greatly changed, usually diminished by as much as half. To avoid this it is simplest for the practitioner to time a comfortable count of four to the nearest second and then, using a watch, to time himself in accordance with this throughout the duration of the exercise, keeping each 'count' of four to the same number of seconds.

In the Golden Dawn it was suggested that the meditations to accompany this exercise should include one in which he or she mentally formulated a cube, endeavouring to discover the esoteric significance of this simple geometrical form, and one in which the practitioner should formulate a crystal of salt 'and entering into it actually feel himself of crystalline formation'.

While this 'salt meditation' is no part of the authentic tantric tradition it can do no harm and may possibly do some good. In the first place it is a useful exercise in visualization, in the second, for reasons connected with tattvic symbolism, it may possibly result in an energization of the Muladhara chakra and even begin the process of the arousal of the serpent power from its slumbers.

A similar visualization of symbols as an accompaniment to pranayama may be employed with the object of vivifying the Svadisthana and Manipura chakras—the energization of these chakras is associated, as was stated on page 60, with, respectively, control of the astral plane and a mastery of magical and alchemical techniques.

With the object of vivifying the Svadisthana chakra the aspirant should practise the four-fold pranayama described above while visualizing himself or herself inside, not a giant salt crystal, but Apas, a giant silver lunar crescent with its horns facing upwards. The object should be to so identify oneself with Apas that one feels one *is* Apas and, in a sense, the quintessence of Elemental Water.

For the energization of the Manipura chakra a precisely similar course should be followed save that the object of identification should be Tejas— a burning-red equilateral triangle, the quintessence of Elemental Fire.

Once the aspirant has reached the point where he can take the identification no further, he or she should endeavour to journey into the realms of Apas and Tejas using the methods outlined on pages 58-59. Those who follow this course will find, at the very least, that they undergo some curiously interesting subjective experiences; some may find that they obtain the supernormal abilities that are traditionally associated with the vivification of the Svadisthana and Manipura chakras.

The next stage of pranayama recommended by the Chiefs of the Golden Dawn was 'Moon breath'—i.e. breathing through the left nostril only. But it seems easier—and is certainly more authentically tantric—to go on to the use of, firstly, a twofold cycle, and then a threefold cycle (inspiration/holding/exhalation) involving the alternate use of each nostril. The procedure is as follows:

1. Close the first and second fingers of the right hand into the palm, place the other two fingers lightly on the left nostril and the thumb on the right nostril, and fill the lungs with air.

2. Close the right nostril with the thumbs and breathe out slowly through the left nostril. Time this exhalation to a period you can manage with reasonable comfort which, depending on the capacity of your lungs and your general state of health, is likely to be between eight and twenty seconds.

3. Breathe in through the same nostril for half the period of the preceding exhalation.

4. Relax the thumb and close the left nostril with the fingers. Perform (2) and (3) above with the right nostril.

5. Continue this alternate breathing until the end of the period of the exercise.

Most people at first find it difficult to persist with this exercise for more than ten to fifteen minutes. In time, however, it is usually possible to be able to carry on for about an hour and to extend the cycle from the first (say) exhalation twelve seconds, inhalation six seconds to, perhaps, exhalation thirty seconds, inhalation fifteen seconds, using, of course, alternate nostrils.

When this has been achieved, or at least approximated to, a threefold cycle can be adopted—ten seconds exhalation, ten seconds inhalation, ten seconds holding. Over a period the length of the various phases of the threefold cycle can be steadily increased, sometimes to thirty or forty seconds. Long before this the practitioner will almost certainly have experienced certain effects, both subjective and objective, of his endeavours.

The immediate (though not perhaps the first) causes of the subjective effects experienced are the changes in brain chemistry induced by alterations in the carbon dioxide content of the bloodstream. Very similar changes can be induced by deliberate hyperventilation, prolonged fast overbreathing, and the subjective consciousness states experienced by a particular person from either 'fast' hyperventilation or 'slow' deep pranayama bear a strong resemblance to one another. As, however, such states are subjective they are marked by personal variation—one experimenter will feel little but mental discomfort and mild confusion of thought, another may experience visual or auditory hallucinations of greater or lesser intensity, still another may experience an uprush of symbolic imagery from beneath the surface of consciousness or even, in some cases, 'mystical bliss'.

According to tantric tradition the four objective physiological results of the successful practice of pranayama are (1) perspiration (2) muscular rigidity (3) Buchari-siddhi, 'the magical power of hopping like a frog', and (4) levitation.

The first and second of these, both of which I have myself experienced, probably result, like the changes in brain chemistry, from reduction in the amount of carbon dioxide in the blood. According to tradition the sweat of pranayama differs from that produced by normal exertion, is imbued with various vital energies and 'subtle airs', and should not be washed off in the usual way but rubbed into the skin as though it were an unguent. If this is done, so it is said, it will be found to be physically, mentally and psychically beneficial. Personally I doubt this, but as I have never tried it I am unable to come to any definite conclusion on the matter. However, it does seem likely that if practised with sufficient regularity over an extended period it will produce the siddhi, magical power, of never having to share a seat on any form of public transport.

The 'magical power of hopping like a frog' is unlikely to be experienced by anyone who is practising pranayama in any sitting posture of a nature found comfortable by a Westerner. It seems to be associated with squatting or kneeling postures and to result from the effects of spasmodic nervous/muscular jerks on a rigid body. As such it should presumably be regarded as being at least semi-pathological rather than a desirable 'magical power'. If, however, the hopping is not the result of muscular spasms but, as is claimed by tantric yogis, the result of an almost total loss of bodily weight, it can be regarded as the first stage of the levitation *siddhi* which some Western yogis, notably Alan Bennett and Aleister Crowley, are alleged to have acquired, at least temporarily, as the result of the employment of pranayama.

Once the practices outlined above have been mastered they can be combined with visualization exercises and, if one so wishes, the use of a mantra or mantras—words and phrases, meaningful or meaningless, which are said aloud, muttered, or mentally repeated, over and over again.

Mantra is a complex subject and one on which authorities differ. Many such authorities affirm that a mantra is utterly useless unless it is pronounced correctly, and that the secrets of such pronunciation are only communicated to a chosen few. The plain fact is, however, that many mantras of Indian origin are used by *both* Tibetan tantric Buddhists and Bon adepts, and that Indians, tantric Buddhists, and Bon devotees *all pronounce them differently*. What is more, each school of Hindu and Buddhist Tantra has its own variations of pronunciation. The situation is somewhat similar to that which prevailed in the Judaism of the dispersion, where, in spite of the emphasis of Rabbinical scholars on the importance of 'correctly' pronouncing Hebrew, 'the language of Paradise', two widely different systems of pronunciation evolved, the Ashkenazic and the Sephardic.

There is no reason to believe that there is the slightest difference between the achievements of Hindu tantrics and Tibetan tantrics, in spite of the fact that the pronunciations, and sometimes the actual form of mantras employed by them are radically different. It is difficult, therefore, to avoid the conclusion that *the way in which a mantra is pronounced is of no real importance whatsoever*.

What, then, of the meaning of a particular mantra?

Once again there has been a great deal of occult mystification on this matter. Mantras do usually have some sort of meaning, although frequently a vague one, but the meanings of them, like those of the 'barbarous words of evocation' used in the Western ritual magic of the grimoires, are the least important things about them. If one chooses to use a traditional mantra, either out of sentiment or of belief in its intrinsic virtue, one is free to do so; but there is no real reason to think, in spite of all that has been said to the contrary, that one mantra is better or more effective than any other—a Western mantra, such as the 'Konx Om Pax' of the ancient mysteries, will be just as much or as little efficacious as an oriental one such as the *Muh Emdap Enam Mau* used by some Bon adepts.

The real value of any mantra arises from its constant repetition and the consequent induction of a dissociation of consciousness. That such a dissociation, sometimes productive of mystical states of a very high order, does take place as a consequence of the use of mantra is a matter of fact. But why should this be so? There is room for disagreement on this matter, but one likely explanation is as follows.

An essential prerequisite for mystical experiences is for the mind to turn in upon itself, to be concerned with the exploration of 'inner space' rather than with the impressions with which it is continually bombarded by the senses. One wants to 'bore' the mind—or, rather, the brain through which the mind interacts with the physical world—so that it turns inward rather than outward. Sensory inputs to the brain are modulated by the reticular system,[1] which controls which sensations reach consciousness. The reticular system becomes habituated to the repetitive stimulation of mantra, its constituent neurones reduce their activity, and the cerebral cortex becomes generally inhibited, thus allowing the mind to turn inward—the prerequisite for mystical experience. This does not mean, of course, that alterations in brain activity are the cause of mystical experiences, tantric or otherwise, but that such alterations prepare the way for such experiences.

Having said this, there are advantages in using traditional mantras rather than, say, the first words of *Little Bo-Peep* or *How Long Blues*. For one thing the use of a traditional mantra may establish a 'psychic link' with those who have used that mantra in the past,[2] for another, the *meaninglessness* of some traditional mantras is positively advantageous—the reticular system is more speedily habituated because the mind does not worry about the meanings of the mantra, explicit or implicit; it simply becomes more and more divorced from the 'rationality' of everyday living, from ordinary sensual inputs, until it is jerked into other modes of consciousness.

There is, in fact, nothing alien to Western mysticism in the use of a combination of mantra and pranayama. The repetition in occult ceremonies of the strange words of evocation to be found in the grimoires is an obvious example of the use of *both* mantra and a sort of 'instant pranayama'. The constant chanting of the long streams of incomprehensible syllables found in such rituals as 'the Invocation of the Bornless One', a sort of deliberate echolalia, results in hyperventilation and consequent changes in blood and brain chemistry.

---

1. The reticular system is spread throughout the brain stem and within it there are two subgroups of neurones, both of which modulate brain inputs. It is the rostral reticular system, at the upper end of the brain stem, which is so responsive to changes in the carbon dioxide level of the blood.

2. In the case of some mantras the establishment of such a link might not be altogether desirable.

Less obvious examples are provided by the vast compilation of Western mystical treatises known as the *Philokalia*, first published at Venice in 1782 but containing material dating from the fourth to the sixteenth century, which includes much concerning 'the prayer of the whole man' which was and is the concern of those Christian mystics known as the Heyschasts.

The Heyschasts, following St Macarius of Egypt—or, to be more precise, the writings attributed to him—have always been concerned with the 'prayer of the heart' rather than 'the prayer of the mind'; 'heart' in this sense meaning all the elements of human totality: soul, mind, will, feelings, and the physical body. The Heyschasts adopted a particular form of words, the 'Jesus Prayer'—'Lord Jesus Christ, Son of God, have mercy on me a sinner'—as a constituent part of their prayer of the heart, repeating it over and over again in exactly the same way in which a tantric yogi repeats Sanskrit mantras. This was usually accompanied by slow deep breathing performed in time to the prayer, in other words, pranayama, and the assumption of a bodily posture of 'inwardness', the head lolling forwards with the chin on the chest and the eyes focused on 'the place of the heart'.

The prayer, the deep breathing with the consequent reduction of the carbon dioxide level in the bloodstream, and the unstimulating character of the posture are all likely to 'bore' the reticular system and produce the cerebral inhibition which is a prerequisite (although not the only one) for the profound alterations in consciousness associated with mystical experience.

It seems fairly clear that pranayama on its own, or the use of mantra on its own, or even, once again on its own, the adoption of a posture in which the senses are starved of fresh impressions, would suffice to produce cerebral inhibition; but that some combination of them would be more quickly effective. There is therefore good cause to use a mentally repetitive mantra—perhaps a very simple mantra such as Om—in combination with pranayama.

It is perhaps worth remarking that while the sensual richness of the Ritual of the Five Ms seems to be in complete contrast with the sensual starvation of mantra and pranayama, both are productive of the same result in purely neurological terms, the partial 'cutting out' of the reticular system. To use an analogy drawn from electro-magnetism—it is no more than an analogy—pranayama and similar techniques render a circuit inoperative by reducing the current flow; the Ritual of the Five Ms achieves the same result by overloading that circuit and blowing the fuse.

Such analogies must not be taken too far, nor must traditional beliefs about the results of the successful employment of pranayama be totally disregarded. According to these the mastery of those basic pranayama techniques outlined earlier in this chapter is the best preparation for both tantric ritual, whether right or left-handed, and for Layayoga, the arousal of the serpent power which lies sleeping 'at the base of the spine.'

Before proceeding to the former, which is dealt with at some length in the next chapter, the latter demands exposition in the context of Western occult techniques.

Layayoga is, as was said earlier, a process which begins with the arousal of the sleeping serpent power in the Muladhara chakra, goes on to raise that power—in tantric symbolism 'the head of the serpent'—through the other psychic centres of the subtle 'body', vivifying each one in turn, and concludes with the explosive marriage of the serpent, the goddess Shakti in her microcosmic manifestation, with Shiva, who dwells in the Sahasrara chakra, the 'subjective Kether' of the Western occultist.

The similar Western process of the Exercise of the Middle Pillar is also concerned with an energy flow, but this is precisely in the reverse direction to that employed in Layayoga and, more importantly, *there is no marriage of Shiva and Shakti,* no orgasmic union of polarities.

The Western occultist who wishes to arouse the power of Kundalini by the use of techniques with which he or she is familiar must, then, not only perform the Exercise of the Middle Pillar in reverse, but aim at something more than the setting up of a flow of subtle energy—the marriage of the force of the subjective Yesod (which subsumes the subjective Malkuth) with the Divine White Brilliance of the subjective Kether.

A suitable exercise for working towards his goal is as follows:

1. Seat oneself in a posture which one finds 'steady and easy', such as that described previously, in which the gods of ancient Egypt were frequently portrayed, but adapt it in such a way that visual impressions are reduced to the minimum possible. Suitable ways of doing this are to focus one's vision on a totally blank wall, or on a totally smooth and blank piece of paper, or, simplest of all, adopting the Heyschast technique of resting the chin on the chest while looking downwards to approximately the bottom of the breast bone.

2. Practise pranayama for ten minutes or so.

3. Continuing to practise pranayama and remaining in one's posture perform *in imagination* the Lesser Banishing Ritual of the Pentagram as given in Appendix D. This incorporates two performances of the Ritual of the Qabalistic Cross, and the 'vibration of Divine Names', which is part of these, can be done verbally, simultaneously

with exhalation phases of the chosen pranayama cycle, instead of in the imagination.

4. Visualize, as strongly as possible, a disk of glowing purple, about four inches across, in the region of the perineum. Continue doing this for five to ten minutes, endeavouring to see the disk in one's mind's eye, and then end the exercise by the repetition of (3) above.

This exercise should be repeated daily until, with almost no difficulty, the purple disk can be visualized so clearly that it is almost as though it was visible to physical sight. How long it takes to reach this stage varies from person to person; those lucky enough to be gifted with the power of eidetic imagination will 'see' the glowing purple disk of Yesod/Muladhara on their first experiment, others will have to persist in the performance of the exercise for weeks, months, or even years.

When this stage has been reached the exercise is repeated daily but with the addition that a yellow square is visualized in the middle of the purple disk and, at the heart of the yellow square, a coiled serpent lying in sleep.

When clarity has been achieved in this visualization, stage four of the above exercise is extended by the other chakras/subjective sephiroth being visualized at their stations in the subtle body. These are, as stated in the preceding chapter, a whirling, glowing gold disk at the non-physical analogue of the heart, a lavender-blue disk at the nape of the neck, and a disk of whirling 'Divine White Brilliance' above the crown of the head. The last can be visualized as being continually receiving an inflow of the 'Divine White Brilliance' from some invisible force. This continual influx is imagined as causing the Kether/Sahasrara disk to overflow and send its energy downwards, like a waterfall of light, to the other three sephiroth/chakras, causing each of them to glow more brilliantly. The waterfall of light is not imagined as entering some sort of 'psychic dam' at the purple disk, but as continuing its vertical flow until it is swallowed up in the earth.

The inflow of energy/psychic waterfall visualization is not an essential part of the Kundalini-arousing exercise, and the 'Divine White Brilliance' conceived of as flowing downwards through the subtle body is not the energy of the serpent-power of Kundalini; it is held to be the energy of the macrocosmic Kether which is being 'tapped' by the microcosmic Kether/Sahasrara and used to stimulate and vivify the entire structure of the subtle body.

When the experimenter has succeeded in his or her visualization exercises to the extent that the various centres, including that which contains the sleeping serpent in its yellow square, can be 'seen' with the mind's eye with almost the clarity of material sight there are two possible courses of action.

The first is to proceed to ritual workings of the sort described in the next chapter. The second is to continue with visualization exercises with the object of arousing Kundalini and causing it to ascend to the Sahasrara.

In the latter case the visualization exercise is continued exactly as previously save that one has to imagine the sleeping serpent as, firstly, stirring, secondly raising its head high and opening its eyes and, finally, beginning to 'stand on its tail' and lift its body upwards through the subtle equivalent of the spine.

This is more easily said or written than it is performed. Most people find it much harder to visualize an object moving in three dimensions than one which is static. Nevertheless, those who have persisted with exercises of this type aver that success is eventually achieved; that this visualization is eventually obtained, *and that then the serpent begins to move upwards independently of the will and imagination of the practitioner*—as though it were endowed with a conscious volition of its own—forcing its way through the various centres until it reaches the Sahasrara chakra and explosively unites with Shiva.[3]

There are various accounts of what is subjectively experienced by the practitioner who reaches this stage. They are interesting but of little real value; the inmost nature of an ineffable experience cannot, by definition, be communicated. But all those who have claimed the experience have been in agreement on one thing. They have been led back to the roots of their own identity and, on every level, the nature of their lives has been transformed into something strange, in a sense otherworldly, but infinitely rich.

---

3. It would seem that there are strong similarities between this experience and that outlined in Taoist treatises concerning 'interior alchemy'. The latter are expressed in crudely physiological terms, as though psychic energies were material things, but the underlying principles would seem to be the same, with Taoist alchemical 'cauldrons' corresponding to the chakras. In this connection see Appendix E.

CHAPTER NINE
Tantric Rituals for Westerners

There are many villages in the prosperous South-West region of England where almost all the traditional thatched cottages are unoccupied from Monday mornings until Friday evenings.

The absentee owners are middle-class Londoners—insurance brokers, journalists, merchant bankers, and so on—who spend the working week in the metropolis but on Saturdays and Sundays feel themselves to be villagers, playing a full part in the life of a rural community. They are usually ready, indeed anxious, to participate in church fêtes, celebrations of national events, such as royal weddings, and other village junketings, and take part in them with gusto. Respectable stockbrokers exchange their grey flannel or pinstripe suits for corduroy trousers and sports jackets with leather-padded elbows and are to be found engaged in such activities as bowling for a pig or grinning through a horse-collar; insurance company executives are seen playing shove-ha'penny and sober financial journalists are to be heard singing songs about jolly ploughboys and their tumbles in the hay with obligingly amorous milkmaids.

It is all completely delightful, completely harmless, and completely bogus. The form is devoid of content, there is no skull beneath the skin; the world which gave meaning to such festivities, as breaks in the hard and bitter work-cycle of the farm labourer, died at some time between 1914 and 1939. There is nothing wrong, of course, in taking part in such solemn mummery—but those who do so in the belief that they are experiencing the same feelings as did, say, a landless labourer at a seventeenth-century Church Ale, are utterly mistaken. The re-creation, however faithful, of a particular form will remain that, and no more, without the (impossible) simultaneous re-establishment of the social environment which gave birth to that form.

The above is as true of religious life as it is of social life. The introduction in recent decades of such features of the worship of the early Church as the kiss of peace and the feast of Agapé into that of contemporary Christian congregations must always remain a vulgar anachronism, an extraordinary attempt to piece together a broken nutshell—while at the same time engaging in the abandonment of the still intact kernel, the theology of the Fathers and Doctors of the Church.

What applies to Christian worship also applies to tantric ritual. It would be perfectly possible for a Western occultist prepared to go to a great deal of trouble and expense to perform the Ritual of the Five Ms in New York or London in exactly the same outward form in which it is celebrated in Bengal or Rajasthan. But this would be to sacrifice the kernel for the shell, content for form, to engage in amateur dramatics rather than to practise an authentic religio-magical technique.

It is an old saying that 'it is not the cowl which makes the monk', and we can be quite sure that it is not the curried beef, the wine, or the employment of a great deal of Sanskrit or Tibetan terminology which makes the tantric adept. If the Ritual of the Five Ms, in either its right- or left-handed incarnations, is to be of use whatsoever to a Western tantric aspirant it must be adapted in one way or another. Tantra is, as has been reiterated throughout this book, a Way of Action; to sacrifice the spirit of Tantra to the letter of an accurate dramatic representation of a Bengali rite would be to abandon deliberate action for mindless automatism.

Most Western tantrics who wish to undertake some form or other of ritual work will find it best to start with a straightforward invocation of Shakti, using the techniques of Golden Dawn ritual magic, before proceeding to rites involving the participation, actual or symbolic, of a sexual partner.

Such a rite may be of a simple nature (there is no need, for example, to emulate the extraordinary complexity of Alan Bennett's rite for the evocation of the Spirit of Mercury which Crowley printed in Vol. 1, No. 3 of his magazine *The Equinox*) but, performed with sufficient enthusiasm, particularly if repeated daily over a period of some weeks, it should prove effective.

The preliminary preparation of one's 'place of worship'—a somewhat pompous occult term for something which, in most contexts, need be no more than the centre of a room normally used for other purposes—involves nothing but a thorough cleansing and the installation of an altar; any small table, or even a wooden box, covered with a clean cloth, will suffice for this purpose.

If circumstances allow, this cloth should be orange-red, a colour traditionally associated with Shakti, and the curtains or other hangings should be of the same colour or, alternatively, they can be of one or more of the 'Binah' colours given in Chapter Three. On the altar should be placed as many Binah symbols (see page 52) as the practitioner chooses—perhaps, for example, no more than a sprig from a cypress tree and/or a bunch of red poppies in a vase—and a delineation of Shakti. This can be symbolic, such as an equilateral triangle outlined in red on a sheet of white paper or an elaborate glyph such as one of the yantras[1] reproduced in books on tantric art—in either case what is symbolized is the vulva of the Goddess, source of all life. On the other hand it can be a piece of representational art, either a statuette of one of the many incarnations of Shakti or a photograph of an old painting of the Goddess. If it is desired to use incense in the course of the rite this should smoulder in a censer placed on the altar before the symbolic, pictorial, or sculpted representation of the Goddess.[2]

Over a period of a week or two preceding the first performance of the ceremony of invocation it is essential that the conventional iconographic form of one of the avatars of Shakti should become so familiar to the practitioner that he or she can visualize it without any great effort of will.

It is best to begin this process of familiarization by buying or borrowing a book containing many illustrations of the Goddess, choosing an illustration which particularly appeals to one but which is not too crammed with the elaborate detail which would make a satisfactory visualization more difficult. The chosen illustration should then be committed to memory so thoroughly that a clear and accurate description of its every detail could be given without once looking at it.

The ceremony proper should begin with a banishing ritual. The Lesser

---

1. A yantra is, literally, 'an instrument'. In the terminology of Tantra it refers to either a geometrical figure or, more rarely, a three-dimensional abstract structure, which is both a cosmogram—a diagrammatic representation of the cosmos on all its discrete levels—and a psychogram, a map of the soul; another aspect of macrocosm/microcosm concept which is common to both Tantra and Western magical theory. The yantra is 'activated' by tantrics through the employment of complex meditative techniques which cannot be satisfactorily used in a Western environment. The complex mandalas of Tibet, which have fascinated many Westerners, amongst them C. G. Jung, are a pictographic extension of the simpler yantra and are used for similar purposes. On the most basic level, which is also the deepest level, all yantras and mandalas are symbols of the vulva of the Goddess, which contains 'all and everything'.

2. Any incense which a person finds 'otherworldly' is suitable—save in evocations to visible appearance incense is employed because of its psychological effects on the practitioner and not because of its supposed physical attributes. Nevertheless, it might be as well if myrrh and civet, perfumes traditionally associated with the Great Mother, were incorporated into any incense used in an invocation of Shakti.

Banishing Ritual of the Pentagram, the rubric of which is contained in Appendix D, is quite adequate for this purpose but any occultist who desires something more elaborate can use the lengthy Golden Dawn banishing rituals of the Hexagram and the Greater Pentagram.

The practitioner now 'enflames himself with prayer'—that is to say, he or she uses Western mantra, which can either be drawn from one or other of the printed versions of those strangely corrupt magical texts known as the grimoires, composed by the practitioner 'according to his or her own ingenium', or adapted from some invocation commonly used by ritual magicians of the Western Esoteric Tradition.

The last is possibly the best, and certainly the most convenient, course to follow. A suitable text for such adaptation is the Graeco-Egyptian invocation known as the Ritual of the Bornless (or headless) One. In occult books written in the English language this is frequently referred to as 'the Preliminary Invocation of the Goetia.' This is a misnomer; the invocation in question was first published in English translation in 1852 and was adopted by the chiefs of the Golden Dawn for their own occult purposes. It has nothing at all to do with the Goetia—which is the first section of a sixteenth-century magical cookbook entitled the *Lesser Key of Solomon the King*—save that Crowley, for reasons best known to himself, chose to print it at the beginning of his edition of the Goetia.

A version of the Ritual of the Bornless One, adapted for the purposes of a Shakti invocation, is to be found in Appendix D. This adaptation consists largely of gender changes—the original Greek text is heavily male oriented and thus unsuitable for use in an invocation of Shakti. The 'names of power', or 'barbarous words of evocation', have been left largely unchanged; although many of them were probably male in their original form most of them have become so meaninglessly corrupted that their *specific* maleness has been lost and they are perfectly usable as mantras in an invocation of the Goddess.

Whatever form of invocation is used the words should be allowed to flow freely whether read or recited from memory. In spite of legends about minor mistakes in the performance of occult rituals resulting in magicians being 'torn to pieces by demons' it does not matter if there is the occasional slip: the whole object of the rite is not liturgical exactitude but the 'enflaming of oneself by prayer'; not formality but fervour.

If the invocation is short, as is the Shakti-adaptation of the Bornless Ritual given in Appendix D, it can be repeated several times. On each occasion it must be accompanied by the visualization technique known as 'the assumption of the form of the Goddess.' This, which is derived from a Golden Dawn method but which is identical in almost every respect with a method used by tantric Buddhists, is performed in the following way.

Practitioners imagine the form of the particular incarnation of Shakti, with which they have thoroughly familiarized themselves in the way described above, *building up around them*; it is as though the individual practitioner's body was at the core of a living status of the Goddess. When the form is built up as fully as possible, which is not difficult for anyone who has practised visualization techniques of the sort described in the preceding chapter, the practitioner visualizes his or her own body expanding and coinciding with the body of the Goddess, filled with her power and dynamic energy. There is no objective way of measuring the extent of the success which has been achieved in the performance of this assumption. All that can be said is that those who have practised such invocations and assumptions affirm that they *know* when success has been achieved: the subjective effects on consciousness are unmistakable. When the invocation has ended, whether in partial or complete success or with no result whatsoever, Shakti is banished by either the Lesser Ritual of the Pentagram or some more complex ceremony. According to Western occult tradition it is important that this should be done at the conclusion of any ritual of invocation or evocation, even one which does not seem to have been in the slightest degree effective. To neglect this is, so it is said, extremely dangerous, even on the level of ordinary life—the man or woman whose psyche is inflated by even a partial identification with some god or goddess is likely to behave in a way so totally at odds with ordinary social conventions that difficulties will inevitably result. In this connection it is interesting to note that Victor Neuburg, the minor poet who is largely remembered for his discovery of the talents of Dylan Thomas, believed that a failure to banish the god Mars at the conclusion of a ceremony of invocation in which he had played the major part was the cause of him behaving in such a way that a woman to whom he was deeply attached committed suicide. Whether or not Neuburg was right in his belief is of no great moment; it is better to be safe than sorry—so to always end a ceremony of invocation with a banishing seems an excellent rule. In any case, the use of a banishing at the beginning and end of a ritual is a psychic 'rite of passage'—the setting apart of the ceremony as something rather especial which transcends ordinary existence.

Those who wish to proceed from invocation of the Goddess to an actual or a 'substitute' working of the Ritual of the Five Ms will find that the following Western adaptation of the rite, with or without the practitioner's own amendments and variations, can be extremely effective.

1. *Place of Working.* Any room which is private and long enough to contain a bed or couch and an altar—any small table—is suitable for celebrating the Ritual of the Five Ms and will be, for the duration of the rite, a Temple of the Mysteries of Tantra.

2. *Time of Working.* There are considerable differences between various tantric schools as to the best time, if there is any best time, for the performance of the rite. The general consensus seems to be that no time is completely unsuitable but that the ceremony is best celebrated during the hours of darkness during a waxing moon. For astrological and qabalistic reasons Western occultists might find it consonant with the symbolism of the Shiva/Shakti polarity to carry out the working on a Monday, a Thursday, or a Saturday. It is worth adding that some Bengali tantrics consider it particularly advantageous to conduct the working at a time when the Shakta—the female partner in the rite—is menstruating. Other groups, however, insist that it should not be performed until five days after the cessation of menstruation.

3. *Temple Furniture.* The altar should be covered with a cloth coloured either orange-red or one of the Binah colours given on page 52. Any curtains or hangings should be of one or more of these colours but, provided that one or more of these is predominant they can be intermixed with one or several of the Chokmah colours as also given in the table on page 52. If the ritual is performed by artificial light it will be best if the electric light bulbs employed are coloured red or violet. Failing this the lampshades should be of these colours, as should any candles used by those who feel these are in some way more authentic than electricity. On the altar, prior to the ceremony, need be no more than a vase containing one or more red flowers, symbolizing the vulva of the Goddess. If it is desired to use incense there can also be a censer containing glowing charcoal.[3] There is no need to go to great expense on either of these points—any glass or metal vessel makes a suitable vase, a red earthenware flowerpot, filled with sand on which stands charcoal, provides an excellent censer and, what is more, one which expresses the appropriate colour symbolism.

4. *The Opening of the Rite.* The participants in the ceremony bring in dishes containing the first four of the Five Ms and place them

---

3. A similar incense to that described above with the addition of musk is excellent. The 'musk' can be a synthetic equivalent of the real and very expensive 'perfume'; the psychological effects should be the same in either case.

on the altar. Those who want to remain fairly traditional can make these spiced cooked beef, a decanter of wine, some variety of sea food—oysters, supposedly aphrodisiac in their effects, would be a good choice—and any vegetable which the participants find excessively stimulating to the palate, dhal cooked with large quantities of garlic and fresh ginger, for example. If one is trying to be as traditional as possible—in the spirit, not the letter, of the tradition—one or more of the Ms should consist of substances of such a nature that the participants would not normally partake of them. If they have been brought up as Muslims, ham can be substituted for beef; if they have never drunk spirits, brandy can replace the decanter of wine; and if they are fanatically opposed to the use of nicotine, some chewing tobacco, or even a packet of high-tar cigarettes, could replace the fish.

If it is planned that the fifth M should be a symbolic, rather than an actual, copulation, then the traditional Ms can be replaced in any way it is wished, provided that there are four things to be eaten, drunk, or even inhaled.

After the four Ms, together with plates and wine glasses, have been placed on the altar the Lesser Banishing Ritual of the Pentagram is performed; only one of the participants should go through the physical motions of the rite, but both participate in it on the level of imaginative visualization.

5.   *The Rite Proper.* The participants in the rite sit themselves on the couch. If substitute workings are in progress, i.e. right-handed Tantra, the woman sits, of course, to the right side of the man; if the rite is left-handed, one which culminates in physical sexuality, the opposite is the case.

In either case the practitioners now endeavour to think of each other as the God and the Goddess, Shiva and Shakti. In right-handed worship this 'divine identification' remains on a fairly abstract level, but in left-handed rites it is very specific, the woman regarding her partner as 'the phallus of Shiva', while she is thought of as being not only Shakta but the living altar on which sacrifice is offered to herself—in the words of one text, held in high regard by many schools of Tantra, 'Her belly is the sacrificial altar, her pubic hairs the sacred grass-mat . . . the lips of her vagina are the sacrificial fire . . .'

In right-handed working the mental processes of identifying oneself and one's companion with Shakta and Shiva is the core of the rite. The four Ms on the altar are partaken of modestly and the ceremony ends with a gift—perhaps a flower or a sweetmeat—

from one partner to the other, this giving being visualized as the embrace of Shiva and Shakti.

In left-handed working, on the other hand, fervour and spontaneity are the essence of the rite. The participants not only identify themselves with the God and the Goddess, but they give the divine forces full play, letting themselves improvise, as the divine polarities inspire them, the feasting, the love play and the copulation of Shiva and Shakti. Within the boundaries of the Temple there are no hard and fast rules—'Exceed, exceed' are the key words, and the Road of Excess leads to the Palace of Wisdom and Understanding and to that Greater Palace which subsumes them.

6. *The Conclusion.* The God and Goddess—for such the participants must now be considered if the rite has been successfully performed—honour each other with a kiss, banish by Pentagram or other rituals, and go their ways.

Working of the above type can only with great difficulty be properly performed by the tantric aspirant. It is true, of course, that anyone not suffering from frigidity, impotence or a gastric ulcer can eat, get mildly drunk, and copulate. But if these things were the essential elements in a left-handed tantric working every tiresome group of suburban swingers engaging in group sex on a Saturday evening would have to be regarded as conducting 'circle worship' of the sort described in an earlier chapter.

In reality, however, the Ritual of the Five Ms is only authentically tantric when *throughout the entire ceremony each participant ceaselessly identifies his or her partner with the God or the Goddess;* this is by no means easy, particularly in the throes of ecstatic copulation with someone to whom one is emotionally attached in their human, rather than their temporarily divine, capacity.[4]

I am told, however, by those I believe competent to judge, that in this, as in mundane activities, 'practice makes perfect.'

---

4. It seems likely that the random choice of a sexual partner, as in 'circle worship', was instituted in order to overcome this difficulty.

CHAPTER TEN
A Summing Up

Tantra is, in its Hindu, Buddhist or Jain versions, totally unsuitable for the use of any Western aspirant who is not prepared almost totally to abandon his cultural and psychic links with his own world and to become what many people would regard as 'an oriental in an occidental body.'

Such a transition is possible, and its results are by no means always unhappy; indeed, some of those who have undergone it have made major contributions to Western understanding of Eastern philosophy, religion and occultism. One thinks, for example, of Agehananda Bharati, the Austrian-born student of Indian language and culture who, after a short spell as 'chaplain' to those few Indian Prisoners-of-War who transferred their allegiance from the Kaiser-i-Hind to Adolf Hitler and his Third Reich, became, firstly, a Hindu *sadhu* and than a tantric Guru, author of *The Tantric Tradition*, a book to which the overworked adjective 'seminal' can be properly applied, even by those, like myself, who regret the influence of linguistic philosophy on the thought of its author.

But the road taken by Agehananda Bharati is one that can be successfully followed by only a few, and most of those who attempt to take it become examples of what Arther Machen called 'the oriental esoteric ass', men and women who either mouth meaningless drivel of the 'tree spreads into the divine Atman and the bul-bul spreads into the *kutcha Shaitain ke-pultan*' variety—a sort of occult Hobson-Jobson—or, even worse, become victims of money-snatching pseudo-gurus of the type splendidly satirized in Gita Mehta's best-selling *Karma-Cola*.

The essence of Tantra, however, is not specifically Indian or Tibetan, Hindu or Buddhist. Indeed, it is not more Eastern than Western: it is as native to Balham or the Bronx as it is to Bengal or Orissa, Rajasthan or Sikkim. It has two aspects.

The first is the recognition of polarity, and the interplay of polarity—on the level of physical humanity, gender and copulation—as the key which unlocks the Doors of Understanding and Wisdom and ultimately leads the seeker to that Crown of consciousness in which the opposites are slain. The second is the acceptance of the fact that the bondage of the senses can be overcome *through* the senses, that there is a Path of Excess which, dangerous as it is for some, can lead to the heights rather than the depths.

This is the real core of Tantra, the fundamental reality of which is not to be found in the use of oriental terminology, the employment of the elaborate symbolic designs of *yantra* and *mandala*, nor even—in spite of much which has been written to the contrary—the initiation of a guru. Tantric gurus abound in India, many of them are either fraudulent or mentally disturbed, and it is extremely difficult for the aspirant to know whether he has found a genuine guru, a glib confidence trickster, or a psychotic. It is safest to avoid all supposed gurus and to rely on the ancient Buddhist tantric tradition that *the sincere aspirant will eventually obtain any initiations that are necessary from a disembodied initiator.* It is worth remarking that each and every one of the great Buddhist exponents of Tantra received an initiation, or initiations, of this sort.

No human being can initiate, in the fullest meaning of the words, another into Tantra—for initiation is an interior process which the aspirant must carry out for himself. Still less can the reading of a book confer some sort of mysterious astral initiation into Tantra. But what a book can do is to outline the nature of the tasks to be performed. Tantra is the Way of Action; it is the following by the individual of a mystic road which leads out of the darkness of time into the light of eternity.

This book is an endeavour to provide a map of that road, an occult psychogram of the path of the senses which leads to the transcending of the senses.

Appendix A
Brodie Innes and The Tattvas

It is possible that, as explained in the note on p. 131, it was not S. L. MacGregor Mathers but J. W. Brodie Innes who made the Golden Dawn summary of Rama Prasad's *Nature's Finer Forces* and the tantric text incorporated into it.

John William Brodie Innes was, as R. A. Gilbert has pointed out, one of the most interesting and scholarly of the early leaders of the Golden Dawn. Born in 1849, a descendant of the Innes of Toux and Pitfour, a cadet branch of the family of Innes of Innes, he was not the first member of his family to practise magic, for one of his forebears not only enjoyed a reputation as a wizard but claimed to have visited Fairyland.[1]

He was, in 1884, one of the founder members of the Scottish Lodge of the Theosophical Society and, in 1890, was initiated into the London temple of the Golden Dawn, later becoming the Imperator of that society's Edinburgh temple, Amen-Ra. Whether or not it was Brodie Innes who made the summary of *Nature's Finer Forces* there is no doubt that he was a diligent student of the tattvic system, and that he spent much time considering its full implications. In 1895 some of the fruits of his tattvic studies were presented to the Scottish Lodge of the Theosophical Society in four lectures. These were later printed in the *Transactions* of that Lodge, but the full text of them is most easily available in R. A. Gilbert's *The Sorcerer and his Apprentice* (Aquarian Press, 1983).

Brodie Innes' lectures seem to me to display not only an enquiring mind and a passion for occultism, but some suggestions of relevance to the study of tattvic theory particularly and occultism more generally.

---

1. Other interesting men remotely related to Brodie Innes include one of the 20 July plotters against the life of Adolf Hitler, William Innes of the Blackheath Golf Club, subject of the best known of eighteenth-century sporting prints, and Gilbert Innes of Stow, friend of Sir Walter Scott.

Brodie Innes, unlike some Western occultists, realized that the tattvas are *connected* with the physical world—the forces, as it were, which exert a formative influence upon it—but are not part of it. The planes of existence he regarded as discrete, not continuous, and he wrote:

This science of the tatwas is not intended to override, or to explain, or to stand instead of, any physical science whatsoever. It does not stand instead of anatomy, or chemistry, or medicine, or biology; it accepts all these . . . to every scientist, in every possible walk of science, the philosophy of the tattvic vibrations says, 'Go on, the more you can find out the better: my science does not conflict with yours in the very slightest degree'.

Brodie Innes was very conscious of the Shiva/Shakti polarity and, in his first lecture, made it clear that each tattva is dual. He emphasized that this duality is not peculiar to the tattvas and, like any tantric, he saw the cosmic polarity as manifested in the physical world. In his own words:

When our world began to revolve upon its axis . . . it generated two centres of force, one positive and the other negative; and it generated a double kind of current, a positive current and a negative current, and these currents really account for most of the physical phenomena of the globe.

Brodie Innes regarded the emotional life of the individual human being as being regulated by the tattvic polarities; their effects, however, being modulated by what he called 'the personal equation', by which he seems to have meant a combination of physical factors, such as bodily health, and the psychological element of 'free will'. He said:

The first tatwa, Vayu, is the gate of motion. When that tatwa is in currency, its effect . . . is to produce restlessness . . . or something of that kind. The following, Taijas . . . produces anger . . . whereas Apas produces receptivity and calm contentment; and Prithivi produces . . . indifference . . . How is it . . . that every human being is not affected with precisely the same moods at precisely the same time? In the first place, because to respond immediately and perfectly to the tattvic current requires absolutely perfect health of every nerve, every ganglion, every cell and every cellule; and secondly . . . you still have to take account of the personal equation . . . Therefore when . . . (a) tatwa comes into play upon the world in general, every human being will respond to it at a different time . . . . But beyond these we have human free-will . . . and not only the free-will of the individual himself, but . . . the will of others as well . . . . Now, for instance, if there be a violent animosity between two persons, the approach one to the other . . . is pretty sure to bring the taijas centres—the centres of heat, anger, and so forth—into strong action to keep those centres functioning even after the taijas current has passed; to retain, so to speak, the taijas vibration circulating throughout the body, and excluding or muting the functions of other centres. And so with all the other emotions, love, and so forth, in precisely the same way.

Brodie Innes' suggestion that, as far as the individual human being is concerned, any tattvic current may be dominant at any time, seems to me of some relevance in relation to the odd procedure, described on p. 84, for deciding the nature of the tattvic tide in flow at a particular time by the random choice of a coloured 'bullet.'

If, as Brodie Innes suggested, the tattvic tide flowing *in an individual* at a particular time can be different from the 'cosmic tide' in flood at that time, there seems to be no reason why that individual should not divine the nature of his or her 'subjective tide' by drawing lots—in this case the lot being a coloured counter or bullet. It could be argued that to take such a course was to follow the basic principle of C. G. Jung's synchronicity—the idea that everything done at a moment of time has the qualities of that moment of time. 'Synchronicity' is, in this context, a fairly new word for the very old concept which underlies such well known Western occult techniques as geomancy and horary astrology.

What seems to be implicit in Brodie Innes' argument is that the 'working occultist' should concern him herself with two sets of tattvic tides, objective and subjective. If, for example, he or she wished to engage in a ritual or meditation particularly consonant with the nature of Apas, he or she would first work out a suitable time by arithmetical calculation (see p. 82) but, when the time came, would if circumstances allowed, only go ahead with the operation if the subjective tide was also of the nature of Apas.

Brodie Innes also made some observations on the relationship between the tattvic currents and clairvoyance. These are of great interest although sometimes marred by an unduly physical presentation of the tattvas. At times, for example, he wrote as though the Tejas tattva and light were identical. It seems quite certain, however, that he really believed that light is a particular manifestation of Tejas, rather as he believed that the body is a particular manifestation of the human spirit.

He also believed that human beings influence one another, for good or ill, through the tattvic forces, writing:

We human beings are constantly forming the prana, the ocean of the tatwas of this earth; and every action that we do not only tends to reproduce the same action in ourselves, but in lesser degree to reproduce the same action in others. Therefore to that extent is every one of us responsible for the moral conduct of every other, because the ocean of prana, through which these tatwas are constantly playing, is formed by ourselves, and is itself the vehicle of the forming of the character of every other human being, forming in fact a network which links us all together.

This supposed network clearly bears some resemblance to two old friends: the Collective Unconscious of Jungian depth psychology and the *Anima Mundi* of the alchemists.

Brodie Innes' approach to astrology was surprisingly tantric—that is, he interpreted it in terms of polarity and tattvic forces. He claimed that:

To know ... the characteristic of the earth ... we have to know the obliquity of its axis, and then to know the exact nature of the Tatwic currents which belong to that plane to which it is polarised. The rules of the old astrologers and the characteristics which they affixed to the star groups give us a great clue ... if you look at the direction of the earth's axis, look at the characteristics of the constellations round the pole star and the characteristics of the constellations round the celestial equator, you will see sorrow, suffering, tribulation, and trial ... On the other hand, look in precisely the same way at the pole of the ecliptic and at the signs of the zodiac ... and you will see the influx of life, rest, peace, and happiness. So you get a key to the characters of systems of worlds and of individuals according to the way in which they are respectively polarised.

While he never used the phrase 'twilight language' Brodie Innes appreciated that the tantric text incorporated in *Nature's Finer Forces* conceals as much as it reveals. He wrote:

There is a good deal in that book which is veiled for exceedingly good reasons, and which no one is allowed to state publicly, for the very sufficient reason that it would give a great deal too much power to people untrained and unfit to exercise such power. That book ... was primarily addressed to Initiates, and to them every sentence is full of meaning, but a great deal is also perfectly intelligible, with careful study, to the outer world.

Brodie Innes believed the tattvic currents to be of such complexity that it is difficult to understand how he thought they could be used in practical occult workings. The sun, he said, is radiating its five tattvas, but so is the earth, and on a different time rhythm. Even more confusingly, every human being 'is radiating its own Tatwas constantly, and those are the Tatwic currents which that human being is conscious of'.

Elsewhere he made it clear that he regarded the tattvic forces as operating on every plane of existence—as the 'formative forces' acting upon the material plane, but also upon the level of mind and spirit. Thus, he said, on the plane of mind:

You get mental activity from Vayu, and mental fire and genius, invention and discovery from Taijas. You get receptivity and the plastic turn of mind from Apas. You get the firm and steadfast mentality, admirably sane and founded upon a rock, from Prithivi. And so you may trace the mental condition of every human being, and you may know precisely what tatwas have operated to produce that particular mind.

Brodie Innes' lectures on the tattvas, presented to his fellow members of the Scottish Lodge of the Theosophical Society almost a century ago, make it apparent that at least some aspects of tantric physiology and cosmology exerted a considerable influence on the early leadership of the Golden Dawn.

APPENDIX B

The Origins of Tantra, Drugs, and Western Occultism

The history of hedonistic mysticism, east and west, can never be fully written. In part this is because the devotees of Tantra and essentially similar European cults have been deliberately secretive about their activities. But, more importantly, centuries of intermittent persecution have destroyed the documentary evidence.

In India such persecution reached its zenith in the thirteenth century when fanatical Muslim rulers, genuinely shocked by what they considered to be the vice and corruption associated with Tantra, murdered the cult's devotees and burned whole libraries of tantric books.

As a result of this and succeeding persecutions—notably one which took place as late as the time of the Emperor Aurungzebe (d. 1707)— no early Hindu tantric books survive, and the earliest known tantric text, which probably dates from the eighth century, is specifically Buddhist.

This does not necessarily mean that Tantra is of Buddhist origin although, quite obviously, there are Buddhist elements in even the most 'Hindu' of tantric texts. It may be that, as has been suggested by several authorities, the origins of Tantra are to be traced to a Dravidian cultural reaction against the beliefs of the Aryan-speaking rulers of ancient India whose religion is expressed in the *Vedas*.

It seems possible, however, that Tantra was influenced by shamanistic techniques involving the use of drugs as means of consciousness enhancement, and that the use of hashish as a preliminary of tantric workings is ultimately a survival of Aryan shamanistic techniques hinted at in the *Vedas*, which are full of references to *soma*, a mysterious 'food of the gods.'

The identification of *soma*, reputed in ancient India to be the food of not only the gods but of those human beings who familiarly commune with those gods, has been the subject of much dispute. At one time it was seriously argued that *soma* was rhubarb root, its purgative properties causing it to be considered divine, but it now seems generally agreed that it was fly agaric, *Amanita muscaria*, a white-spotted red toadstool which, taken in small doses, induces trance and visions. In larger doses it is lethal.

While hashish and other cannabis derivatives are not such effective hallucinogens as fly agaric, they are undoubtedly safer and, in many parts of the world, have been used by shamans as a substitute for *Amanita* and other 'magic mushrooms'. It may be that a substitution of this sort—hashish for *soma*—can be discerned in left-handed tantric practices.

Indian attitudes towards the use of hashish and other hallucinogens—save alcohol—have usually been tolerant. It is the beef eating, wine drinking, and sexuality associated with Tantra that are shocking to orthodox Hindus, not the use of cannabis.

In Europe the situation has been quite otherwise, and the general attitude, shared by most occultists, has been one of intense disapproval of the use of hallucinogens. Dion Fortune, for example, regarded them as psychologically and physically dangerous, claiming that the use of them resulted in 'psychic obsession' and was 'bad for the heart'. There seems to be little evidence in support of the latter claim as far as most hallucinogens are concerned, while the evidence for the former is purely anecdotal. This does not mean, of course, that the possibility of psychic damage can be totally disregarded and, in any case, the use of many hallucinogens is illegal in both North America, the UK, and continental Europe.

Most, although not all, Western occultists who have taken a favourable attitude towards the use of consciousness-altering drugs have been influenced by Aleister Crowley. Crowley's favourite hallucinogen was mescal, which he claimed to have introduced to Europe; certainly he included it amongst the ingredients of the 'loving cup' he administered to the participants in the 'Rites of Eleusis' which he celebrated in Edwardian London, while one of Crowley's former disciples—almost certainly the only man who had both played first-class County Cricket and evoked the god Thoth-Hermes to visible appearance—told me that, in pre-Hitler Berlin, Crowley gave mescal to, amongst others, the youthful Aldous Huxley.

There is no record of Crowley ever having used *Amanita muscaria*, fly agaric, but there is some slight evidence that he may have known of its consciousness-altering properties.

The evidence in question is one of Crowley's paintings, used as the frontispiece of Vol. III, No. 1, of his magazine *The Equinox*. In the background of the painting is portrayed an ecstatic woman dancer; in the foreground stands a dead tree, from a branch of which a corpse is suspended by the neck—a common symbol of the transition from one state of consciousness to another. From behind the tree peers a grinning nature spirit, standing guard over what are quite clearly both the common red and the rarer gold varieties of *Amanita*. This spirit has been given the features of C. G. Jones, a chemist and student of pharmacology who introduced Crowley to the Golden Dawn. It seems at least possible that the implication of this is that Jones had known of the properties of *Amanita* and had introduced Crowley to them. Unfortunately there are no extant records of Crowley's drug experiments during the years from 1898 to 1911, when the two men were closely associated.

If Jones had been a participant in these experiments, as was, quite certainly, Alan Bennett of the Golden Dawn, it is possible that his curiosity concerning hallucinogens had been aroused by his reading of alchemical and magical literature, of which he was a dedicated student—there are passages in such works as *The Magus* (1801) and *Theatrum Chemicum Brittanicum* (1652) which I think refer to processes designed to extract hallucinogens from plant and animal substances. If I am right in my supposition, there are traces of an underground European occult tradition involving the use of hallucinogens—which does not mean that (apart from any questions of legality) the use of such substances as a technique for consciousness alteration is intrinsically desirable.

There is, in fact, a far stronger argument against the use of 'psychedelic drugs' than any used by Dion Fortune and other non-Crowleyan Western occultists. This argument is summed up in a Latin phrase used, in quite a different context, by several scholastic philosophers: *Quidquid recipiteur secundum modum recipientis recipiteur*, 'What is received is in accordance with the nature of the receiver.'

This tag can be applied to many situations. To the reader of any tantric text, for example—from these and similar 'open texts' the reader will receive what is in accordance with his or her nature.

In the context of the use of the hallucinogens the phrase is of equal relevance. Shamans, tantric adepts, and others who have gone through long preparatory processes may find them useful, 'giving' what has been worked for, and is, in a sense, 'already there.' Those who have not engaged in such preparation—extending, perhaps, over many years—will not obtain some instant illumination. On the contrary, they are likely to experience nothing but a welter of confused images, valueless at best, at worst resulting in some form of pathological psychic disturbance.

APPENDIX C
The Chod Rite and Asiatic Shamanism

It seems possible that the Chod ritual is a re-enactment, on a psycho-spiritual level, of a shamanistic ceremony involving the seeming self-mutilation and miraculous bodily healing of the practitioner.[1]

There survive several European accounts of ceremonies. The following, which originally appeared in the Abbé Huc's *Travels in Tartary, Thibet And China During The Years 1844-1846*, is clearer than most and is particularly interesting in that the ceremony was conducted in a Mongolian monastery which was at the time reported to be controlled by members of the 'Black Hat' Karmapa sect—strongly influenced by both left-handed Tantra and the old Bon faith. Father Huc wrote:

A Lama was to cut himself open, take out his entrails, and place them before him, and then resume his previous condition. This spectacle, so cruel and disgusting, is very common in the Lamaseries of Tartary. The Boktè who is to manifest his power, as the Mongols phrase it, prepares himself for the formidable operation by many days of fasting and prayer, pending which he must abstain from all communication whatever with mankind, and observe the most absolute silence. When the appointed day is come, the multitude of pilgrims assemble in the great court of the Lamasery, where an altar is raised in front of the Temple gate. At length the Boktè appears. He advances gravely, amid the acclamations of the crowd, seats himself upon the altar, and takes from his girdle a large knife which he places upon his knees. At his feet, numerous Lamas, ranged in a circle, commence the terrible invocations of this frightful ceremony. As the recitation of the prayers proceeds, you see the Boktè trembling in every limb, and gradually working himself up into phrenetic convulsions. The Lamas themselves become excited; their voices are raised; their song observes no order, and at last becomes a mere

---

1. Thubten Jigme Norbu, elder brother of the present Dalai Lama, has made the curious suggestion that it is the Chod ceremony which is the original and the shamanistic rite which is the imitation; this, surely, is to put the cart before the horse.

confusion of yelling and outcry. Then the Boktè suddenly throws aside the scarf which envelops him, unfastens his girdle, and, seizing the sacred knife, slits opens his stomach in one long cut. While the blood flows in every direction, the multitude prostrate themselves before the terrible spectacle, and the enthusiast is interrogated about all sorts of hidden things, as to future events, as to the destiny of certain personages. The replies of the Boktè to all these questions are regarded by everybody as oracles.

When the devout curiosity of the numerous pilgrims is satisfied, the Lamas resume, but now calmly and gravely, the recitation of their prayers. The Boktè takes, in his right hand, blood from his wound, raises it to his mouth, breathes thrice upon it, and then throws it into the air with loud cries. He next passes his hand rapidly over his wound, closes it, and everything, after a while, resumes its pristine condition, no trace remaining of the diabolical operation, except extreme prostration. The Boktè once more rolls his scarf around him, recites in a low voice a short prayer; then all is over, and the multitude disperse, with the exception of a few of the especially devout, who remain to contemplate and to adore the blood-stained altar which the saint has quitted.

Father Huc added that he did not believe 'there is any trick or deception' associated with 'these horrible ceremonies', that 'the devil has a great deal to do with the matter', and that 'our impression there is no trick ... is fortified by the opinion of the most intelligent and most upright Buddhists whom we have met in the numerous Lamaseries we visisted'.

The question of whether the exercise involved any deception—pious prestidigitation of the type of allegedly involved in some medieval European miracles involving the liquefaction of clotted blood—is of no real significance to the question of the origins of the Chod ceremony. Even less germane is the question, raised by Father Huc, of diabolical intervention. What to me seems certain is that shamanistic rites of the type described above are the ancestors of the sophisticated Chod ceremonies of Buddhist Tantra.

APPENDIX D

Preparation for the Middle Pillar Exercise and Shakti Invocation

The rubric of the Lesser Banishing Ritual of the Pentagram, mentioned on p. 117 in connection with the 'reverse Kundalini yoga' technique known as the Exercise of the Middle Pillar, is divided into four parts and is as follows:

The ritual should begin facing East. The gestures are performed with the right hand. The lines should either be traced with a steel dagger or with the sign of benediction. To form the sign of benediction extend the first two fingers, whilst covering the last two with the thumb.

1. *Qabalistic Cross*
a. Touch the forehead and say ATEH (*thou art*) ('Ah-teh')
b. Touch the breast and say MALKUTH (*the Kingdom*) ('Mal-kooth')
c. Touch the right shoulder and say VE-GEBURAH (*and the Power*) ('Vay-geb-or-rah')
d. Touch the left shoulder and say VE-GEDULAH (*and the Glory*) ('Vay-ged-you-lah')
e. Cross the hands on the breast and say LE-OLAM (*to the ages*), AMEN. ('Lay-orh-lahm, Ar-men')

   Whilst performing this the practitioner should strongly visualize the hand as drawing a line of white light through the crown of the head, pouring into the body, and descending to the solar plexus, and from there to the feet, the microcosmic location of Malkuth. Also draw a line of light from the right shoulder to the left shoulder whilst saying 'Ve-Geburah, Ve-Gedulah', thus forming a cross. At the centre of this cross visualize a rose, either natural or in the stylized form of the rose-cross, when vibrating 'Le-Olam, Amen.'

   This completes the so-called 'Qabalistic Cross'.

2. *Inscription of Pentagrams*
For the purpose of the Lesser Banishing Ritual of the Pentagram the type of pentagram used is the pentagram of Earth, thus:

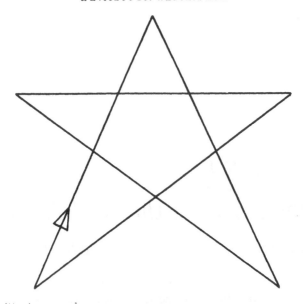

This is inscribed in the air by keeping the arm straight and bringing the hand from the vicinity of the left thigh to a point level with the forehead and then back to a position near the right thigh, thus inscribing an inverted 'V'. Then, bring the hand up to a point just left of the body at the same height as the shoulders. Draw it across in front of the body to the same shoulder height position at the right side of the body. Complete the pentagram by returning the hand to the left thigh position.

When proficiency is gained with the movements, they can be synchronized with the breathing, taking an in-breath for an upwards stroke, an out-breath for the downwards strokes, and holding for the cross-stroke.

a.   Still facing the East inscribe the first banishing Earth pentagram, then taking an in-breath as you draw your hand back to your chest, stab the centre of the pentagram and vibrate the Godname, YHVH (Pronounced Ye-ho-wah) using the full out-breath.

b.   Keeping the hand extended, turn to the South, repeat the same process and vibrate ADNI (Ah-doh-nai).

c.   Then turn to the West, repeat the process and vibrate AHIH (Eh-he-yay).

d.   Finally turn to the North, repeat the process and vibrate AGLA (Ah-gla) then with hand still outstretched, return to the East.

The main visualization work for this section of the ritual is to see the lines of the pentagram cut in the air and flaming so intensely that anything beyond them diminishes in intensity, thus focusing the practitioner's attention on the limits of the circle which his hand has traced whilst turning from quarter to quarter with his hand extended. As each Godname is pronounced imagine it carrying to the very limits of the Universe, in the quarter in which it is vibrated.

3. *Invocation of the Archangels*

Extend the arms in the form of a cross and proclaim:

'Before me, Raphael (Rah-fay-el)
Behind me, Gabriel (Gab-ray-el)
On my right hand, Michael (Mee-Kay-el)
On my left hand, Auriel (Or-ray-el)
For about me flames the Pentagram,
And above me shines the six-rayed star'.

The visualizations that are most important for this sector of the ritual are the anthropomorphic shapes of the Archangels.

To the East, Raphael, Archangel of Air, is seen towering above the practitioner robed in yellow which as it rustles in the breeze blowing from the rear of the figure flashes with purple overtones, flickering across it like the colours on shot silk. He holds a Wand.

To the West, Gabriel, Archangel of Water, holds aloft a Cup from which flows water. His robe is of shimmering blue with overtones of orange.

To the South, Michael, Archangel of Fire, is clothed in robes of red, flashing with the complementary green, holds aloft a flaming Sword.

To the North, Auriel, Archangel of Earth, is clad in the colours of the seasons, rich and fertile, citrine, olive, russet and black. He stands on a Pentacle.

The last two lines re-affirm the presence of the Pentagrams (which are then re-visualized) and the hexagram (Star of David) which is visualized above the circle.

4. *Qabalistic Cross*

This completes the ritual cycle, and is a repeat of the first section.

The adaptation of the so-called 'Preliminary Invocation of the Goetia', to which reference is made in Chapter Nine in the context of the Invocations of Shakti, is as follows:

The Invocation of the Bornless One

Thee I invoke, the Bornless one.
Thee, that didst create the Earth and the Heavens.
Thee, that didst create the Night and the day.
Thee, that didst create the darkness and the Light.
Thou art Jabas:
Thou art Japos:
Thou art distinguished between the just and the Unjust.
Thou didst make the female and male.
Thou didst produce the Seed and the Fruit.
Thou didst form men to love one another, and to hate one another.
Thou didst produce the moist and the dry, and that which nourisheth all created Life.
Hear Me:
Ar: Thiao: Rheibet: Atheleberseth:
A: Blatha: Abeu: Ebeu: Phi:
Thitasoe: Ib: Thiao.

Hear Me, and make all Spirits subject unto Me: so that every Spirit of the firmament and of the Ether: upon the Earth and under the Earth: on dry Land and in the Water: of Whirling Air, and of rushing Fire: and every Spell and Scourge of the Goddess may be obedient unto me.

I invoke Thee, the Terrible and Invisible Goddess: Who dwellest in the Void Place of the Spirit:

Arogogorobrao: Sothou:
Modorio: Phalarthao: Doo: Ape, The Bornless One:
Hear Me: etc.
Hear Me:
Roubriao: Mariodam: Balbnabaoth: Assalonai: Aphniao: I: Thoteth:
Abrasar: Aeoou: Ischure, Mighty and Bornless One!
Hear me: etc. [as above].
I invoke Thee:
Ma: Barraio: Joel: Kotha:

Athorebalo: Abraoth:
Hear Me: etc [as above].
Hear me!
Aoth: Abaoth: Basum: Isak:
Sabaoth: Iao:
This is the Queen of the Gods:
This is the Queen of the Universe:
This is She Whom the Winds fear
This is She, Who having made Voice by her Commandment, is Queen
    of All Things: Ruler and Helper.
Hear Me, etc. [as above].
Hear Me:
Ieou: Pur: Iou: Pur: Iaot: Iaeo: Abrasar: Sabriam: Do: Uu: Adonaie: Ede:
    Edu: Angelos ton Theon: Anlala Lai: Gaia: Ape: Diathanna Thorun.
I am She! the Bornless Spirit! having sight in the Feet: Strong, and the
    Immortal Fire!
I am She! the Truth!
I am She! Who hate that evil should be wrought in the World!
I am She, that lighteneth and thundereth.
I am She, from whom is the Shower of the Life of Earth:
I am She, whose mouth ever flameth:
I am She, the Begetter and Manifester unto the Light:
I am She, the Grace of the World:
'The Heart Girt with a Serpent' is My Name!

Come Thou forth, and follow Me: and make all Spirits subject unto Me so that every Spirit of the Firmament, and of the Ether: upon the Earth and under the Earth: on dry land, or in the Water: of whirling Air or of rushing Fire: and every Spell and Scourge of the Goddess may be obedient unto me!

Iao: Sabao:
Such are the Words!

APPENDIX E

The Siddhas, Chinese Alchemy, and Layayoga

There are some resemblances between the theoretical aspects of Tantra and the ancient Indian Siddha cult. The main emphasis of this latter movement was on a psycho-physical yogic process designed to achieve spiritual development through an intense physical development supposedly leading to a vast extension of the life-span or even actual immortality. The cult, which in somewhat altered form survives at the present day, holds that 'death may be either put off *ad libitum* by a special court of re-strengthening and revitalizing the body so as to put it permanently *en rapport* with the world of sense, or be ended definitively by dematerializing and spiritualizing the body, according to prescription, so that it disappears in time in a celestial form from the world of sense, and finds its permanent abode in the transcendental glory of God.' This immortality is to be achieved by 'drinking' the 'nectar' dripping from the 'moon' in the thousand-petalled lotus, the Sahasrara chakra.

It is probable that the Siddha cult evolved out of ancient Indian alchemy, which, like later Western alchemy, was not purely a primitive chemistry but was an amalgam of a physical *praxis* with mystical techniques and speculations having some similarity with those of Tantra. According to Dr V. V. Raman Shastri there was an ancient vernacular tradition that the Siddhas were 'a band of death-defying theriacal and therapeutic alchemists indebted in all respects to Bhoga, a pre-Christian Taoist immigrant from China.' It is likely that there was a certain amount of truth in the traditional belief that the doctrines of the Siddhas had a Chinese origin, for a sexo-yogic alchemical school putting great emphasis on the prolongation of life survived in China proper until the Communist takeover in 1949, and at the present time it still has living adepts in Hong Kong and amongst the overseas Chinese of South-East Asia.

The date of the origin of alchemy in China is uncertain, but it was clearly very early, tradition averring that it was first practised in the fourth century BC by a certain Dzou Yen, a magician whose miracles included ripening millet in a cold climate by playing music on a set of warm pipes.

As early as 144 BC an imperial edict forbade the manufacture of alchemical gold—on the ground that unsuccessful experimenters turned to robbery and murder in order to regain the wealth they had squandered—but the prohibition does not seem to have extended to the search for the pill of immortality; for only eleven years after the prohibition the Emperor gave a friendly reception to an alchemist who claimed to have discovered the secret of eternal life by worshipping the Goddess of the Stove.

An early test lays down the pre-conditions for achieving success in the practice of alchemy; the practitioner must fast for a hundred days, he must not be born under unfortunate planetary configurations, he must learn the art orally, from a Taoist master—books being only for beginners—he must worship the gods in a fitting manner, and, above all, he must not be a civil servant. In spite of the semi-magical, semi-religious conception of the nature of alchemy that underlies these rules there is no doubt that at this early stage of the evolution of Taoist alchemy the manufacture of the elixir was still supposed to be achieved by a manipulation of physical substances.

By the end of the sixth century AD *physical* alchemy in China was in a state of decline; by the end of the first millennium it was all but extinct. From it, however, using much of its chemical terminology and many of its theoretical concepts, evolved a number of closely related schools of interior psycho-spiritual alchemy in which the *ting* (the cauldron), the furnace, the lead and mercury that were to be transmuted into the gold of immortality, were all considered as component parts of the human practitioner of the art. At least one, and probably all, of these Taoist alchemical schools was largely concerned with sexuality and the generative process.

There is a curious dichotomy in both the Indian and Chinese attitudes to male sexuality. On the one hand sexual potency—indeed sexual athleticism—is regarded as being a desirable male attribute. On the other hand, semen is regarded as something very precious, something that must not be wasted, and many men worry that they may be suffering from a quite imaginary disease called spermatorrhoea—an involuntary leakage of semen supposedly leading to physical and mental debility or even to death. This conception of semen as concentrated life-force, loss of which should at all costs be kept to a minimum, is not peculiar to the Far East but seems to be a widespread human belief, emanating from the deepest levels of the unconscious, and it is only in the last few decades that it has ceased to be part of the popularly accepted sexual wisdom of the West.

The teachers of Chinese sexual alchemy have been (and still are) quite as convinced of the evil effects of the loss of semen as were our Victorian ancestors; the mere production of the fluid in the body leads to harmful results—thus a chapter of one text urges abstention from onions, leeks, and garlic on the grounds that they are aphrodisiac and encourage the production of 'generative fluid' while another section of the same instructional work argues that the untimely deaths of elderly people occur because they have allowed themselves to continue enjoying sexual intercourse, thus letting the 'generative fluid' leak away and leaving them with no 'vital resistance' against infection. In spite of the crudeness of such physiological conceptions it would be unfair to dismiss Taoist alchemy out of hand, for beneath the primitive biological beliefs and terminology is concealed an extremely subtle psycho-spiritual philosophy and technique designed to harness and transform the forces of the libido in order to attain adeptship—the 'manufacture of the elixir of immortality'.

Chinese sexual alchemy conceives of semen as a physical product of what it calls 'generative force'—the 'essence of procreation' which has some resemblance to the libido of the depth-psychologists and more to the orgone energy of Wilhelm Reich. The first step in the process of manufacturing the pill, or elixir, of immortality is the prevention of the generative force from following its usual course (i.e. the production of semen) by the 'lighting of the inner fire'. This is done by a type of regulated and deep breathing very similar to the pranayama of Indian tantric yoga. The breathing in brings pressure to bear on the generative force, which is situated in a crucible (i.e. a centre of psychic force more or less identical with a chakra) in the lower abdomen, and causes it to rise up a psychic channel associated with the spine to the top of the head. The deep expiration of the breath then brings the force down through the (psychic) channel of function at the front of the body back to the crucible from whence it came. The process of circulation is continued until the generative force is considered sufficiently purified to be ready to be transmuted into *lead*—which in this connection means something like the prana, vital energy, of Tantra—and then it moves up from the crucible, or psychic centre, in the lower abdomen to that situated in the solar plexus, where the transmutation takes place.

It must be emphasized that in the process briefly described above sexual excitation as such is not avoided; however, ejaculation *is* avoided and the force of sexual excitation is supposedly taken to be used in the creation of lead (vitality). Indeed, a total lack of *any* sexual excitation is considered to make the alchemical processes quite impossible of achievement; the Taoist master Chang San Feng said that in the case of elderly people who felt no spontaneous sexual arousal the practice of masturbation was a useful means of stimulating the generative force. He recommended that after the elderly male practitioner of alchemy had achieved an erection by this means he should commence the deep breathing exercises and visualization of the circulation of the force and continue this process until the penis ceased to be tumescent—this cessation of erection being regarded as evidence that the alchemical agent (the generative force) had successfully been transferred to the psychic centre in the solar plexus.

After the successful transmutation of the generative force into lead (prana) the next stage is to raise the lead from the solar plexus crucible to the psychic centre associated with the head (supposedly situated in approximately the same position as the pineal gland) where it is to be transmuted into mercury (i.e. spiritual force) by yet another series of exercises involving deep breathing and the visualization of orbiting streams of force.

The Taoist alchemical texts inform the student that, when this has been achieved, nocturnal emissions—the much-dreaded spontaneous loss of semen and the 'magical' type force associated with it—will cease; he is warned, however, that when he has reached this happy state 'prenatal vitality' will escape from the bowels in the form of wind. The breaking of wind is regarded as desirable when the wind is merely noxious gas evolving from decomposing food in the stomach and intestines, but the would-be alchemist is warned not to break wind if the 'wind' is really 'prenatal vitality' and detailed instructions are given to him as to how this occurrence can be prevented. They involve placing the right middle finger on the 'dragon centre' (the end of a psychic channel supposedly terminating in the palm of the left hand), simultaneously placing the left middle finger on the 'tiger centre' (a similar psychic channel terminating in the palm of the right hand), raising the tongue to the palate, contracting the anus and taking seven deep breaths. This procedure, students are assured, will spread vitality throughout the body and eliminate the tendency to break wind.

In Taoist alchemy the eyes are regarded as positive (yang) and the rest of the body as negative (yin). Therefore when the vital force has been raised to the psychic head centre it is by rolling the eyes in a particular manner that the practitioner achieves the 'inner copulation' that supposedly leads to the manifestation of spirit. This rolling of the eyes is performed in cycles of sixty—thirty-six times from left to right and then twenty-four times from right to left (in Taoism thirty-six is a yang number and twenty-four is a yin number). Each revolution of the eyes is done slowly, being accompanied by a full inspiration and expiration of the breath.

When spirit has manifested in the head centre it is driven down to the crucible in the lower abdomen (sometimes referred to as 'the water centre') in order to be 'fixed' and stabilized. When this has been done the mercury (i.e. stabilized spirit) is enveloped by lead (vitality) which has previously been purified by being vibrated in a continuous ascent and descent of the psychic channel that links the psychic water centre with the psychic fire centre situated in the heart. The united lead and mercury form what is sometimes referred to as the immortal embryo.

The alchemist now begins to practise 'immortal breathing', often referred to as the self-winding (i.e. automatic) wheel of the law. This is done by accompanying every inspiration of the breath with the visualization of a stream of force entering the body at the heels and travelling up to the brain and accompanying every expiration of the breath with a visualization of the same force travelling down from the brain and out through the trunk. This leads to the production in the head centre of a divine food which nurtures the immortal seed situated in the water centre. The alchemical process is completed; all that remains is the quickening of the immortal embryo with spirit—another complex set of exercises enables this to take place—and the alchemist becomes ready to undertake the final stage of the work.

When the immortal seed has been nurtured to maturity—this is indicated by six signs—the alchemist is ready to prepare the elixir of immortality. Guarding himself against destroying all that he has previously achieved (such destruction comes if the alchemist indulges in any one of the 'seven passions', the 'ten excesses', or the 'nine unsettled breaths') he gathers together the 'four essentials of alchemy'—utensils, money, friends, and a suitable place. The utensils are simple enough; a rounded wooden 'bun', covered in cotton, used to block the anus, and a clothes peg to put upon the nostrils. The money is required for the mundane purpose of purchasing food, the friends (who must also be alchemists) are required to attend to the physical needs of the practitioner and 'to pinch his backbone when required'. The ideal place is an ancient Taoist temple on a mountain, far away from either cities or graveyards; 'it is advisable to choose an ancient abode where previous masters have realized immortality so that it is free from disturbing demons and the practiser can enjoy spiritual protection from his enlightened predecessor', said Chao Pi Ch'en.

Having reached to his temple the alchemist concentrates on the lower abdominal (water) centre and 'shakes the six sense organs' (nose, ears, eyes, tongue, mind, and penis). This 'arouses the immortal seed' in the testicles and it tries to move out through the penis. This exit, however, has already been shut by the exercises previously performed by the alchemist and the immortal seed now moves towards the anus; here its escape is prevented by the previously mentioned wooden bun. The whole object of the exercise is to cause the immortal seed *to travel up the spine.* When the alchemist feels the seed approaching the coccyx he 'opens' the spine by (1) pressing a finger hard on the base of the penis, (2) rolling his eyes, (3) sucking in a deep breath, (4) thrusting his tongue against his palate, and (5) stretching the small of his back.

Simultaneously one of the companion alchemists pinches the base of the backbone and the immortal seed passes through the first 'gate of the spine'. The immortal seed then passes up the spine through two other gates (at each of which the five dragons sequence is again practised) to a psychic centre situated at the back of the head.

Immediately the immortal seed has reached the head the practitioner begins an eye-rolling sequence—thirty-six revolutions from left to right and twenty-four revolutions in the opposite direction—all the time gazing at the inner light that now manifests itself. The immortal seed, prevented from escape via the nostrils by the use of a clothes-peg now moves down into a psychic cavity situated above the nostrils and is passed down the body into the lower abdominal centre. There it remains; the alchemical operation is complete. Immortality has been achieved and the alchemist has only to develop his (immortal) potentialities and to appear in countless 'transformation bodies'.

In spite of the crudely physiological way in which Chinese sexual alchemy is expressed in its treatises—perhaps a deliberate 'blind' designed to mislead the unwary—it is clear that the 'attainment of immortality' is something very like the Shiva/Shakti marriage of tantric Layayoga.

It is difficult to believe that the two systems are not derived from a common ancestor—a sort of 'proto-Tantra'.[1]

---

1. For the handful of readers of this book who may get a sense of *déja-vu* on reading the above I should explain that is partly based on a chapter in *Il Cammino del Serpente*, a long out-of-print book written by myself.

Select Bibliography

Anand, Mulk Raj, and Mookerjee, Agit, *Tantra Magic* (Arnold Heinemann, Delhi, 1977).

Arundale, George S., *Kundalini: An Occult Experience* (TPH, Adyar, 1962).

Avalon, Arthur (see under Woodroffe, Sir John).

Bharati, Agehananda, *The Tantric Tradition* (Rider, London, 1965). [Contains an excellent bibliography.]

———, *The Light at the Centre* (Ross Erikson, New York, 1976).

Bhattacharya, Benoytosh, *Introduction to Buddhist Esotericism* (OUP, 1932).

Blofeld, John, *The Way of Power* (Allen and Unwin, London, 1970).

Cavendish, Richard, *The Magical Arts* (Arkana, London, 1984).

Chakravarti, Chintaharan, *The Soma or Saura Sects of the Shaivas* (Calcutta University Press, 1932).

Crowley, Aleister, *Bagh-i-Muattar, the Scented Garden of Abdullah the Subtle Satirist of Shiraz* (privately printed, London, 1910).

———, *The Book of Lies* (Wieland and Co., London, 1913).

———, *777 Revised* (Neptune Press, London, 1951).

———, *Confessions* (Jonathan Cape, London, 1969).

———, *Crowley on Christ* (C. W. Daniel, London, 1973).

Dasgupta, Shashibhusan, *Obscure Religious Cults* (Calcutta University Press, 1946).

———, *Introduction to Tantric Buddhism* (Calcutta University Press, 1950).

David-Neel, Alexandra, *Initiations and Initiates in Tibet* (Rider, London, 1932).

———, *The Secret Oral Teachings in Tibetan Buddhist Sects* (Mahabodhi Society, Calcutta, 1950).

Devi, Kamala, *The Eastern Way of Love: Tantrik Sex and Erotic Mysticism* (Simon and Schuster, New York, 1977).

Douglas, N., and White, M., *The Black Hat Lamas of Tibet* (Luzac, London, 1975).

Eliade, Mircea, *Shamanism: Archaic Techniques of Ecstasy* (Routledge and Kegan Paul, London, 1964).

Evans-Wentz, W. Y., *The Tibetan Book of the Dead* (OUP, 1928).

———, *Tibetan Yoga and Secret Doctrines* (OUP, 1935).

_____, *The Tibetan Book of the Great Liberation* (OUP, 1954).

_____, *Tibet's Great Yogi Milarepa* (OUP, 1956).

Fortune, Dion, *The Mystical Qabalah* (Williams and Norgate, London, 1935).

Garrison, Omar V., *Tantra the Yoga of Sex* (Julian Press, New York, 1964).

Gilbert, R. A. (ed.), *The Sorcerer and His Apprentice* (Aquarian Press, Wellingborough, 1983).

Goswami, Shyam Sundar, *Layayoga* (Routledge and Kegan Paul, London, 1978).

Govinda, Lama Anagarika, *Foundations of Tibetan Mysticism* (Rider, London, 1959).

Guenther, Herbert V., *Life and Teachings of Naropa* (Clarendon Press, Oxford, 1963).

Hirst, Desirée, *Hidden Riches* (Eyre and Spottiswoode, London, 1963).

Hoffman, Helmut, *The Religions of Tibet* (Allen and Unwin, London, 1961).

Jaggi, O. P., *Yogic and Tantrik Medicine* (Atma-Ram, Delhi, 1973).

James, E. O., *The Cult of the Mother Goddess* (Thames and Hudson, London, 1959).

Kale, Arvand and Shanta, *Tantra: The Secret Power of Sex* (Jaico, Bombay, 1976).

King, Francis (ed.), *The Secret Rituals of the OTO* (C. W. Daniel, London 1974).

_____, *Il Cammino Del Serpente* (Edizioni Mediterranee, Rome, 1979).

_____, *The Magical World of Aleister Crowley* (Weidenfeld, London, 1977).

Krishna, Gopi, *Kundalini: The Evolutionary Energy in Man* (Routledge and Kegan Paul, London, 1971).

_____, *The Awakening of Kundalini* (Dutton, New York, 1975).

Kumar, Pushpendra, *Shakti Cult in Ancient India* (Bhartiya, Varanasi, 1974).

Lal, Kanwar, *The Cult of Desire* (Asia Press, Delhi, 1966).

Maraini, Fosco, *Secret Tibet* (Hutchinson, London, 1952).

Mathers, S. L. MacGregor, *Astral Projection, Ritual Magic and Alchemy* (Enlarged Aquarian Press edition in preparation).

Mookerji, R. K., *Rasa-jala-nidhi: or Ocean of Indian Chemistry and Alchemy*, 5 vols. (Calcutta University Press, 1926-38).

O'Flaherty, Wendy, *Asceticism and Eroticism in the Mythology of Shiva* (OUP, 1973).

Pandit, M. P., *Kundalini Yoga* (Ganesh, Madras, 1978).

_____, (compiler), *Gems from the Tantras*, 2 vols. (Ganesh, Madras, 1969, 1970).

Payne, Ernest A., *The Saktas* (YMCA Publishing House, Calcutta, 1933).

Rambach, Pierre, *The Secret of Message of Tantrik Buddhism* (Rizzoli, New York, 1978).

Rawson, Philip, *Tantra: The Indian Cult of Ecstasy* (Thames and Hudson, London, 1974).

_____, *The Art of Tantra* (Thames and Hudson, London, 1974).

Regardie, Francis Israel, *The Golden Dawn*, 4 vols. (Aries Press, Chicago, 1937-40).

_____, *The Art of True Healing* (Helios Books, Toddington, 1964).

_____, *The Middle Pillar* (Llewellyn Publishers, St Paul, 1971).

_____, *The Complete Golden Dawn System of Magic* (Falcon Press, Phoenix, 1984).

_____, *The Foundations of Practical Magic* (Aquarian Press, Wellingborough, 1979).

Sastry, K., *The Veda and the Tantras* (Ganesh, Madras, 1951).

Schoterman, J. A., *The Yonitantra* (Manohar Publications, Delhi, 1980).

Sellon, Edward, *Annotations on the Sacred Writings of the Hindoos* (London, 1865).

Sharpe, Elizabeth, *Secrets of the Kaula Circle* (Luzac, London, 1936).

Sinha, J., *Sakta Monism: The Cult of Shakti* (Calcutta University Press, 1966).

Snellgrove, David L. (ed.) *The Nine Ways of Bon* (Routledge and Kegan Paul, 1981).

Tucci, Guiseppe, *The Theory and Practice of the Mandala* (Rider, London, 1961).

Vliet van, C. J., *The Coiled Serpent* (Navajivan Press, Ahmedabad, 1963).

Walker, Benjamin, *Sex and the Supernatural* (Macdonald, London, 1970).

_____, *Man and the Beasts Within* (Stein and Day, New York, 1977).

_____, *Tantrism* (Aquarian Press, Wellingborough, 1982). [Contains an excellent bibliography.]

Watts, Alan W. (ed.), *The Two Hands of God—The Myths of Polarity* (G. Braziller, New York, 1963).

Wayman, Alex, *The Buddhist Tantras: Light on Indo-Tibetan Esotericism* (Routledge and Kegan Paul, London, 1973).

White, John (ed.), *Kundalini: Evolution and Enlightenment* (Doubleday, New York, 1979).

Woodroffe, Sir John, *The Great Liberation* (Ganesh, Madras, 1951).

_____, *The Greatness of Shiva* (Vedanta Press, Hollywood, 1953).

_____, *Shakti and Shakta* (Ganesh, Madras, 1953).

_____, *Garland of Letters* (Ganesh, Madras, 1953).

_____, *Principles of Tantra* (Ganesh, Madras, 1955).

_____, *The Serpent Power* (Ganesh, Madras, 1958).

Index

TANTRISM
ITS SECRET PRINCIPLES AND PRACTICES

Benjamin Walker. Reveals Hinduism's left-hand path — the most extraordinary belief ever to have come out of India. Dozens of tantric sects use spells and psycho-sexual rituals as a short cut to occult knowledge and magical power. Benjamin Walker charts the strange and — by Western standards — often sickening customs of this amoral religion, which helped to shape events in Hitler's Germany and is influencing today's punks, rockers and skinheads. According to tantrik medieval writings, we have now entered mankind's last age — *kali yuga* — when wealth rules and spiritual, mental and physical diseases are rampant.